D1685440

The
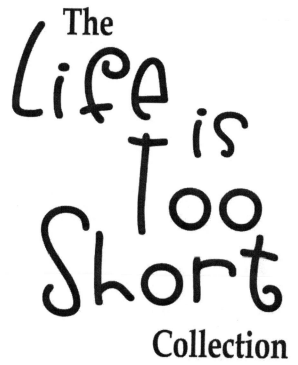
Life is Too Short

Collection

Connie E. Sokol

PRAISE FOR *THE LIFE IS TOO SHORT COLLECTION*

"It didn't take long for Connie Sokol's new book to bring me relief. I wasn't even finished before I felt renewed. Every woman needs to read this and be blessed by her wisdom and humor. Life can be simpler and happier. She has the formula. Thank you, Connie!"

—Joy Lundberg, Co-author of *I Don't Have to Make Everything All Better*

"LOVED. LOVED. LOVED it! Captivating and inspiring, you will laugh, you will ponder, you will plan, you will rejoice. And then you will be ready to take on life again."

—Shauna Wheelright, Book Reviewer, I Love to Read and Review Books

"Every page reminds me of Erma Bombeck as Connie dares us to laugh at ourselves (and to forgive ourselves too) for loving our kids too much and measuring ourselves too harshly. If you have any doubt on your ability to make the most of marriage and motherhood, this will be the book that will help you believe again. But, keep the tissues nearby you'll need them to wipe away your tears from laughing!"

—Rebecca Cressman, KSL Radio Host

The Life is Too Short Collection

CHAWTON PUBLISHING

WOODLAND HILLS, UT

Connie E. Sokol

© 2013 Connie E. Sokol

No part of this book may be reproduced in any form whatsoever without prior written permission of the publisher except in the case of brief passages embodied in critical reviews and articles.

ISBN: 978-0-9890196-5-1

Published by Chawton Publishing, 865 S. Oak Dr., Woodland Hills, UT 84653

Cover design by Kelli Ann Morgan
Cover design © 2012 by Connie E. Sokol
Typeset by Heather Justesen

THE LIFE IS TOO SHORT COLLECTION

WOMAN

I. Enjoy the Journey

II. Dreams for the Journey

III. Goals for the Journey

MOTHER

I.   Reach for the Ideal

II.   Patient with the Real

III.   Help Children Grow

IV. *Make Sure They Know*

WOMAN

ENJOY THE JOURNEY

LEARNING TO RELAX

After chatting with several friends over the past few days about relaxing, I have realized yet again that we women are WOUND. Do you feel that way? Do you wake up with a knot in your stomach or feel like you're walking on eggshells, waiting for the penny to drop, the clock to strike, the disaster to hit? A friend I talked to said that during a typical conversation with someone, the other person said, "Why are you clenching your fists?"

This is a rational, nice woman who openly confesses that she is wound (which, of course, wouldn't be any of us).

Living this way is not only tough on our bodies and emotions but is a one-way ticket to panic attacks, primal screams, alienating all known forms of friends and losing our hair.

So what do we do about it? Stop right there. It's first and foremost *not* about doing.

We women are stellar at *doing*. Suppose we try doing nothing for about five seconds? Then perhaps the next time we can draw that out to ten seconds, and with luck and some classes, perhaps even a full minute.

Quite seriously (though not too seriously because I am not wound), here are some thoughts (that I really need to follow).

Take an actual "time" time-out. One friend said that she literally sent her husband and many children to their annual Disneyland trip *without her*. This was completely intentional. For the first time in a very, very long while, she had the house to herself (didn't she want to run through it, dancing in her bathrobe?). It was joy. It was divine. It was sublime. Of course they came home and she then she was back to cracking out the B12s as fast she could open them but *those four days were fabulous*.

Next, breathe. When your son says he has a broken foot, the teacher calls and says you have to bring him RIGHT NOW to finish official and very vital state testing, your baby has thrown up on you, your husband forgot his cell phone and needs you to drive it an hour away while you forgot the spaghetti noodles boiling on the stove, and because of the stench you all have to live in the basement for two days, HEY, BREATHE.

Truly, there are all kinds of boring statistics on how fabulous, utterly fabulous, breathing well and deep is for the soul. So right now as you read this, sit up tall, and breathe from your diaphragm, in through your nose for five seconds, out through your mouth for five seconds. Do that three times. Afterwards, you have either passed out or feel great—but either way, you're in a better place, right?

Remember, life is one day at a time. Though planning ahead is a great skill, we women can get too ahead of ourselves and squelch the fun—and the growth. In my smug way of trying to prevent all forms of accidents and bad choices for my children, I inadvertently ruin many a good teaching moment. This is mostly because I hate inconvenience and, bottom line, life is inconvenient (refer to broken foot child which occurred as a natural consequence to a choice that I would have usually prevented).

Keep in mind that we can only live life in 24-hour increments. We actually only live minute to minute, but that freaks me out and I am not mature enough to handle it. So I consider 24 hours—I only have to be kind, to be patient, to be a great mother for 24 hours. Then tomorrow I can give 'em heck. But for today, I can relax. Because all my notes are on the calendar and in my planner and I have to ENJOY the process, enjoy that the wind is howling outside and making me feel cozy as I write this; enjoy that my baby is sleeping contentedly; enjoy that my son is wanting yet another snack (the one with the broken foot, who has now been christened Little Lord Fauntleroy).

My job for today is to LIVE, and hopefully, to LIVE WELL; simply that. I can enjoy loving my children, stopping and looking at the sky, tasting a bit of delicious chocolate, laughing at my 3-year-old's antics, lying on the floor and breathing (see prior step).

If you're reading this and feeling relaxed, congratulations! You are allowing yourself to let go already. If, however, you are gripping the side of the book or nervously pulling at your face or hair, I invite you to reread this essay, this time lying on the grass, looking up at the sky...

THE REALITY OF LIVING
IN TWO REALITIES

Lately, I've been thinking about realities. Like the reality that you have four pairs of fabulous jeans in the closet but you can only fit into one. Or the reality that you deeply love your children, and yet today you want to physically rip out their vocal cords if they sass you one more time. This is a complex issue—this living in two different realities—the one reflects a woman who is the best in us, and the other a woman who's "working on it."

Sometimes we can look at others and see their best reality. Their children are excellent students and they're not even trying. Or their finances seem to flow like endless waters and they're not even budgeting, while your reality is scraping life together and barely making ends meet. Or view the "best reality" woman whose child seems to win all the school contests, or is the type of mom who knows exactly where her Children's Tylenol is kept. I once attended a meeting at a woman's home when in the middle of her sentence her adult daughter called and asked her mother how long to boil a soft-boiled egg.

And she knew.

Sometimes this can make our "working on it" reality-self feel a little stressed. I'm not going to share a happy thought here that this is actually a good thing, that seeing our striving self brings needed humility, or that it helps us feel compassion and connection with others. I'm simply making an observation about what *is*, and that we save time and stress (ours and others') by openly acknowledging it.

For example, years ago our family was asked to sing in church. We chose a song about families loving and helping each other, and hoped the message would subconsciously seep into our children's formative brains. The children's performance was beautiful. So much so that afterward many friends approached us and expressed many kind sentiments. After thanking them, I added, "You should have seen us three hours earlier."

Because you see, three hours before our performance, the scene in our home went like this: My husband was at a meeting, so I was the lone parent, running around checking each child's various stages of wardrobe "readiness". Most of them were playing with toys, or hide-and-seek with their shoes. When I called our six children down to practice the song, the older boys said something like, "This is totally preschool and I'm not doing it." On top of that, the younger children couldn't sit still long enough to remain in a permanent line. And due to the anxiety of it all, I kept sweating off my makeup.

The joyous high point hit when my sons finally sat down on the sofa but refused to sing at all, and I yelled at them to get up and see it through to the end, or some such motivational phrase. Yes, *yelled at them*, to sing a church song. A family-loving-each-other church song. That's when I started to cry.

So you can see why, as each person thanked me and looked at me with that "Gee, what a wonderful family" gaze, I wanted to pull down a mammoth white screen and replay for them the previous three-hour tour.

This experience has stayed with me a long time (though therapy has somewhat helped). Because now when I see an obvious "best reality" in someone else, before I allow my "working-on-it" self to feel guilty, I remember a perfect song and the imperfect three-hour tour that preceded it.

And that brings me back to a reality I can live with.

BLAST SUPERWOMAN
INTO HYPERSPACE

When we were first married, my husband experienced many health problems. Wanting to be the "good wife," I took over both our roles and did everything, twice, with footnotes. One night my husband said, "Honey, please go to bed."

I replied, literally crawling on the floor, "I just need to fold a little more laundry."

Over the years this sort of twisted overworked-martyr approach has earned me Oscars in the "Wow, you are amazing" category. But it's taken a few health problems myself to discover that Superwoman needs to hit hyperspace, and that being amazing is completely overrated.

There are two reasons for this. First, it alienates you from others. This bizarre standard on some alien measuring stick puts being incredible over being vulnerable, a key ingredient for love (and sort of important in relationships). Every time women walk into your home and see candles flickering, dishes done, and bread cooling, emotionally they're reaching for a brownie. A big one. Soon, the thought of talking to you gives them hives.

Try being un-amazing by being vulnerable. This is not "dumbing down," faking humility or acting talent-less. It's about showing your soft underbelly, being just as candid about locking keys in the car as getting the Guggenheim. Being un-amazing is letting people in the door even when the dishes aren't done.

Second, being amazing skews your perspective. I've seen women on decorating committees debate napkin colors like they were negotiating world peace. We develop microscope lenses—instead of seeing clearly, we focus deeply on one part. Rather than see the big picture, we see what we focus on, in 1,000x magnification. Try living with that for two weeks. To be un-amazing, let it go.

JoAnn Larsen, author of *I'm a Day Late and a Dollar Short and It's Okay*, says, "Give up perfectionism, you have to give up ... the notion that you really could be perfect in some area if you try hard enough. The truth is you can never be perfect in this life—anywhere, ever."

Ask yourself, "Is it really important? Is it crucial to life's happiness?" If a women's committee wants green napkins with fuchsia plastic flowers, great. Let go of unnecessary control and reclaim normalcy.

Being un-amazing is not the same as blah. *Blah* is wearing your thin, once-was-terrycloth robe, or eating Rocky Road straight from the carton—with fingers. *Un-amazing* is potential without great stress. As soon as you lift the extreme expectations, you can breathe. It's light, free, motivating. Suddenly you can't wait to do what five minutes before you justified avoiding, simply by changing your expectation.

If you struggle with a Superwoman in your closet, kick her out, permanently. Allow yourself to be vulnerable and let go of unnecessary stress. Unless, of course, they want green napkins with turquoise plastic flowers; now that's worth fighting.

FEEL MORE JOY IN WOMANHOOD

Sometimes I observe women—at the grocery store, the park, the playground. And the posture I most often encounter is one I've affectionately deemed as the "Mom Stance." Hands on hips, furrowed brow, and NO SMILE. It plagues us all, this serious business of daily living. One woman was lamenting her perceived failures and what she could do better, when her daughter said, "You could smile, Mother, you could just smile."

So what would help us smile, get the joy back, and feel juiced about life as a woman, wife, and mother?

Be Yourself, Be Your Best Self. Why are we women so consumed with looking sideways for approval? Patricia T. Holland says in her book, *On Earth as it is in Heaven*:

"[God] uses us because of our unique personalities and differences rather than in spite of them. He needs every one of us, with all our blemishes and weaknesses and limitations."

Ask for heavenly help to see your unique strengths and abilities, without comparing yourself to the Neighbor with the Size Two Waist. Chieko Okazki in her book, *Lighten Up*, shares about the time when she moved from Hawaii to teach in Utah. Being of Japanese descent—and it not being too long after World War II—she was concerned about possible negative reactions. Sure enough, it wasn't very long before the principal called and said three parents asked for their children to be withdrawn from her class. She didn't stress, get mad, or eat a cheesecake. Instead, she played to her strengths. After making a bright fuscia-colored dress with matching bow, she stepped out confidently onto the playground, gathered her awestruck class, and loved them like her own. Later the principal said that the three parents had asked for the children to be reinstated. Then she said, "But I told them, opportunity only knocks once."

Find a Personal Purpose or Passion. Women are natural creators, and many experts even encourage us to be so. Find what you like to do. If you don't like scrapbooking, don't do it! No Eleventh commandment says, "Thou must delight in doo-dads." Whether it's painting, singing, photography, or raisin-jewelry making, find what brings you joy, then share it. One friend emailed to tell me that she is participating in the New York City Marathon this fall, pushing the wheelchair of a disabled friend. Find time for things that bring you joy and you'll be a happier, healthier woman and mother.

Have Fun! When was the last time you remember having non-productive fun? Last year I was invited to speak at a women's conference in Hawaii. My husband and I decided to take our high-school graduate son for his senior trip. Out of all the amazing and fantastic things we did together that week, his favorite experience was "When you and dad and I were getting tossed in the sand and the waves". He reveled in seeing us have fun body surfing (also known as teenage recreational torture).

11

What makes you laugh, feel happy, and release those happy endorphins? Maybe it's a no-chores Friday, or ending housework at 5 p.m., or actually swinging on the swings with your children at the park (and telling them to pump their own legs!) Delight in the day. Find the perk and you'll find the joy. Forget being a martyr and start having more fun in daily life.

Give one of these tips a try. Joy is a conscious choice—if we look for it, ask for it, and delight in it, we will find it. Often. And usually in the most simple and delectable of things of life.

BEING LESS INTENSE

We were readying to leave on our big once-a-year family vacation to Oregon. This is the time when not only do we hang out, relax, and enjoy, but it's also a sixteen-hour drive, each way, with eight people in a Suburban. For some that may signal scary. For me, it signals Golden Writing Time as I type in the front seat.

But—wrench in the plan—my goal for July was to "Just Be." Hmmm. In a state of conflict right before we left, I nervously eyed my laptop, charged and ready to go. Could I truly pass up such a great opportunity for uninterrupted type/read/organize time, simply to Just Be???

Thankfully, principle won out. For the first time in a long time, I literally left my laptop at home without a backward glance. And though I brought a tote stuffed with the latest self-improvement books, I left it untouched. Instead, I savored reading the entire Harry Potter series all the way there and back, talking over key plot points with my son.

I had also left my part-time business in the care of talented women and I did not look back. In a place with no cell phone coverage, I truly and literally let go.

Ironically, while reading I learned a great deal. I had felt fearful about an upcoming conference presentation that was being taped and would be seen by potentially 40 million people. NO BIGGIE. I happened upon the part in *The Goblet of Fire*, before Harry was to meet the dragon, and I felt myself work through it like he did. Therapy by Harry!

If you're finding yourself wound, feeling intense about life and what needs to get done, may I encourage you to carve out and then *take* some totally nonefficient time? During the car ride, I almost felt guilty (for the first ten minutes) that I wasn't doing something productive. Then, it felt absolutely fabulous.

Put off something productive—just once—and do something totally silly, purposeless, and not "on your list." This nonproductive time might produce more than you realize.

SQUEEZE THE GUILT SPONGE

I was at Barnes and Noble studying, researching, and minding my own business. After a brief walk around the store, looking at new titles, I returned to my original table loaded with my own books brought from home to read when I saw an employee picking up extra books on various tables.

Immediately, I wondered about my own texts—would the employee understand that these stacked books were mine, previously bought right here at Barnes and Noble, and not ones I was trying to pilfer? Suddenly, I was overwhelmed with guilt. Even though I had truly purchased those books—the receipt was somewhere at home or in the dog's kennel—this did not matter. I was flooded with anxiety. *She's going to think I didn't buy them and now she's going to yell THIEF in front of everyone in this store, and they will stone me with thick biographies.*

Continuing in this ridiculous paranoia, I walked to the front counter to pay for two books I was now purchasing—not from guilt, of course. I hesitantly asked the cashier, what if, say, I really had bought some books before tonight but didn't have my receipt and had brought them with me right now, but I thought the store people, she, might think I had really stolen them. She blinked. I took it to mean she thought I was a thief. She slowly said to just relax, as if I had an Uzi in my purse, and suggested I keep future receipts in the books.

It was forty-five minutes of total stress, on MY NIGHT OUT, about something that wasn't true but that I felt guilty for.

Ever felt that?

My guilt wasn't related to non-stolen books but to all things I have done and not fessed up to. Criminal things, like retelling a story and saying it was Walnut Street, and then later realizing it was Pine Street. Or even worse, parking in front of the Do Not Park sign to return a movie.

I quote wise words from "What About Bob?": there are two types of people in this world—those who like Neil Diamond and those who don't. And there are two types of guilt: healthy and pointless. Healthy guilt prompts you to change wrong behavior. Pointless guilt prompts you to eat a box of Ho-Hos. With pointless guilt, you say one thing but think another and mentally carry on several guilt-chats while having a real-life conversation (which, incidentally, annoys real people involved in the real conversation).

It's time to squeeze the guilt sponge and let the guilt drain out. To do this, try one thing: Say to yourself, "I am not perfect." It sounds simple, even brainless. ("Well, of course I'm not perfect.") And yet simple things are usually the hardest to practice because of their apparent ease—things like, eat well, exercise regularly and get adequate rest. No-brainers, guaranteed success, and yet still we say, "Oh yes, I really *should* do that."

This week try this no-brainer: When you lock yourself out, burn the lasagna, or forget your son's appointment, stop before launching the guilt attack. Laugh and say, "I'm not perfect!" and give the guilt sponge a satisfying squeeze.

TAKE THE LONELINESS
OUT OF BEING ALONE

When I told an inquisitive acquaintance I was taking a weekend holiday unaccompanied, she said, "ALONE? Just you? By yourself?" After assuring her I was somewhat familiar with the meanings of unaccompanied, I thought more about her surprise, shock, utter astonishment. *What was so unthinkable to a woman, I wondered, about being alone?*

When posing that question to a few other women, a friend told me she felt rejected when alone. It reminded her of being back in third grade watching kids pick a four-square team, and standing there, not the last picked, just unpicked. Alone. Another friend said it felt like an open admission that she has no friends, that she is unlikable, and that when walking around by herself she wears an invisible scarlet A: "Alone."

I too have secretly worn this invisible scarlet A, sitting alone at a craft class or scrapbooking night, listening to all the close-knit groups of twos and threes with bobbing heads and occasional peals of laughter. To my friends I say I enjoy going alone, to people watch, to hear the chatter and stories. But sometimes, I'm back in the lunchroom holding my tray, desperate for an empty chair by someone I vaguely know from an algebra class, but smiling as if all is going as planned. The crime of being alone without someone is what makes 35-year-old women still walk to the bathroom together.

This week, try being alone. Take an hour or two (stop your whining, yes you can) and go somewhere you like—the mountains, a park, perhaps a bookstore if you're not ready to break with humanity altogether. Take a book, or some paper, or close your eyes and listen. Allow your thoughts to roam free without putting up fences like, "that reminds me I need to," "I forgot to," "I have to." I'm talking about thoughts like, "What do I want in life," "What do I love to do," "How can I share who I am?" Answers to these questions are worth savoring, pondering, even writing down.

Being alone reminds us to be still, to feel and to listen—and the ripple effect spills right into our relationships. No matter what frustrating circumstances prompted the need, I'm not five minutes into my alone time when I feel a surge of gratitude for my husband, my children and my life. As you allow yourself time to be with yourself, you automatically do the same for others. When your husband wants to go fishing, you are not alarmed, nor angry. You understand his need to be alone and to be quiet because you experience and fill that need too.

The other day I heard my two sons debate over building a Tonka city when my oldest paused and said, "No, I need some alone time right now." Unlike me in middle age, he in childhood is better at understanding when he needs to play, be alone, and hopefully walk to the bathroom unaccompanied.

DOING MORE THAN ENDURING

Do you ever feel that, as a mother, you are an Enduremeister? Often I see mothers believe that we are the only ones who can get something done, and because of previous experience supporting that fact, we continue in this belief.

A while back I had a pivotal experience. A particular Monday and Tuesday were to be, in all ways, nightmares. Monday morning I had a photo shoot in a distant city, then a segment on a major news show. On Tuesday, I was guesting on a TV show then a radio show, and after that, hosting my own show for an hour.

Yes, just thinking about it gave me hives.

To add to the adventure, I needed my hair done. Being a tomboy of sorts, I put off this little time-waster as long as possible. But in trying to confirm my appointment, the stylist could not be reached. For three weeks. In desperation I called a new gal at the same salon and arranged to do hair at 7:00 A.M. on the nightmare Monday morning.

The choreography that went into this Herculean schedule change I cannot describe. Between my husband rearranging his schedule, coaching children to get ready while I was gone so that I could return, have breakfast together, get them on the bus, *and* ready my things for this photo shoot, it would truly boggle the mind.

I rose early at 6:30 A.M. on the fateful morning, after the night that my baby woke up EVERY HOUR.

Finally, at 5:00 A.M. I realized she had stuck pieces of paper and bits of crayon up her nose some time during the previous day. In the dawn's early light, I sat with tweezers and her head between my feet to pull out the contraband. At 6:45 A.M., with nary an hour of sleep, I drove in the chilly weather to get my hair done.

The stylist didn't show.

I sat waiting, with great hope and optimism and many calls, but nothing. In fact, even days later, nothing. I am inclined at this point to share the name of the salon but will refrain.

This shot the whole plan. My bangs, practically down to my nose, were in serious need of cutting or I would have to curl them into the "wall of bangs." By the time I got the kids off to school and the young ones in the bath, I had fifteen minutes to do my hair and makeup, then load up to be in time for the photo shoot.

Now, the whole point of my sob story is this: I still thought I could do it. Even when I looked at the time and clearly saw that it would be ridiculous to even attempt it, I still thought, "I can do it. I can do my makeup on the freeway as I drive. I can put rollers in my hair and drive with them in. I can drive in my pajamas and dress at the studio."

Yes, insanity had set in.

At that point I literally burst into tears and went to my only place of solace—the bathroom. After I sat for a few minutes and collected myself, I realized the following: (a) hair is annoying; (b) this was not essential; and (c) people may mock me on the news for the wall of bangs, but what does it matter?

I came out a different woman. I called the photo shoot guy, explained the hair trauma, and we rescheduled. It was that simple. Instead of flying around, stressing everyone out, with one simple phone call we were back to normal. I spent the morning happily with my children until it was time to go. And with the aid of an entire can of spray, the hair ended up being doable.

Sometimes I think we mothers are so used to enduring, of adding one more thing and feeling the responsibility to make it work, that we don't STOP and ask, is there a simpler way? When we look at all that could be done, why not remember: (a) WE don't have to do it all, and (b) it doesn't all have to be done.

Next time you or I encounter such chaos, we can ask ourselves if there is a simpler way. And maybe we'll find we can do more than endure.

SOMETIMES LIFE IS LIKE THAT

The other morning began like this ... the children were late getting up (despite my coaxing) because of the "summer is in the air, don't want to go to bed" syndrome (or so I thought).

I had been up life coaching online until midnight when my baby, who was starting a cold, woke up and would not go back to sleep. Exhausted, at 3:00 A.M., I passed the baton to my husband, while my other daughter decided to play musical beds until 5:00 A.M.

Exhausted, I corralled the children downstairs for breakfast. Pulling down the Cheerios I realized someone had left the bag open and down came the rain of cereal over literally half the kitchen floor. As soon as I cleaned it up, while getting cereal for the other children, my four-year-old bumped her cereal bowl, creating one of those splattery, upturned, it goes everywhere messes, on the other side of the kitchen floor (and kitchen table, and kitchen chairs).

Cleaning this up—with gentle, encouraging phrases like "YOU'RE GONNA MISS THE BUS, HUSTLE YOUR BUSTLE NOWWWWW"—I realized that the chores from last night had not been completed. My daughter couldn't find the "right" shirt to wear and was in a tear-filled breakdown, and my other son who had sworn to finish his homework had instead joined everyone else and AT THE HAND OF THEIR FATHER listened intently to a sports game on the radio downstairs (the penny drops on the non-chore doing).

23

By this time, the Nazi in me had taken over and I began barking commands: "HAIR, GEL .... YOU. BACKPACK, SNACK... NO TREATS. YOU—SHOES ARE NOT AN OPTION AT SCHOOL."

And then I heard that sound that makes us all freeze in mid-air—the sound of a rumbling school bus passing our driveway. In one of those classic mother moments that you swear you will never experience, I said in an I-told-you-so yelling tone, "YOU'VE MISSED YOUR BUS. GET YOUR FANNIES TO THE STOP SIGN AND STAY TOGETHER."

Ahh, family togetherness.

The point of this is that it's been a week. And though most of the time it's working, unbelievably and in a way I can't fathom, sometimes, like yesterday, it goes to the dogs (or the kitchen floor).

So my thought here is two-fold: life's moments aren't always going to be balanced and beautiful, even when you're practicing balanced and beautiful principles (or even teaching them, creating products about them and talking about them on TV or radio). Because, as you know, there would be no growth, and that would be boring—never mind give me nothing to write about.

So, in tribute to mothers everywhere, thank you for your unspoken patience in *days like that*, and support of what all mothers do—especially for me as a cereal-cleaning, command-barking mother.

WOMAN

DREAMS FOR THE JOURNEY

FAITH IN YOUR DREAMS

I had finished speaking at a once-a-year, week-long women's conference that gathers about 30,000 attendees. As I savored the experience of being a part of such an amazing week for women, I thought back to about six years and 30 pounds previous—when I was a sleep-deprived, dream-deprived woman who spent way too much time hiding out in her fat pants—and marveled at what had taken place.

Because of this, I share a thought about having faith in your personal dreams—the ones that you hold deep in your soul but don't allow to fly.

When my children were babies, I desired to share messages of value to women. But it seemed out of my reach for many reasons—exhaustion, fear, lack of time, you name it. And all of these affected my personal desires.

Yet step by step, I moved forward. I read a little here, spoke a little there, applying these concepts to my own marriage and family, and before you know it, I was doing and living the dream, the very life that I had envisioned but was afraid would never have.

Dear ladies, DO NOT GIVE UP ON YOUR DREAMS, whatever they may be! Whether it's a healthy marriage, secure finances, painting or writing— whatever it is—do not think for a second you can't do it. Of course you can. You will simply need to muster some energy, faith, and wisdom to make it happen.

Recently, I learned this again when I organized a "Weekend for Women," a large local one-day conference for women. I was thrilled that Fox News called to say we would be on their program the day before the conference to talk about it. Although my mother and another company board member were flying in that morning, I thought I could quickly squeeze in this helpful promotion opportunity.

That morning I decked out in my suit and even my fat tourniquet (those "body sizers" that about suck your lifeblood) and began the drive to the city. En route I received a beautiful and apologetic call from the show's producer saying they had to cut the spot that morning because they had one anchor out on illness and three other live shots (which would be near impossible to do with only one remaining anchor). She had pored over the schedule to allot us even two minutes of air time, but said she was still two minutes over without us being on.

I told her that I completely understood and was about to hang up the phone when I got a feeling of peaceful hope. So I said to her (being my bold self) that if things changed, I had my cell phone on me and that I would be at the airport (which HAPPENED to be right by the Fox Studios).

As I drove to the airport, I considered changing out of that uncomfortable fat squeezer and into jeans that I had also brought but the thought came, *Show a little faith here.* So I stayed in my suit.

I picked up my mother (the flight was EARLY—who has heard of that?) and the other lady was right on time. We had barely left the airport when Fox News called and said, "By the way, we have had some cancellations and have a few minutes open. Are you interested?" We whipped a U-turn and laughed ourselves silly while I drove, trying to find the right street to get back on the highway, and my mother and friend fluffed my hair and refreshed my makeup.

We arrived and I literally ran from the car through their backdoor, where I was shown to the studio, and went on live! It was an amazing experience that demonstrated to me the power of faith.

Putting one step forward and pursuing your dream is powerful stuff. It doesn't matter your age, situation, hair color, or shoe size. Your dream matters and it CAN come true. You must be willing to make the commitment to it. It doesn't matter if it takes one year or ten years, it's worth all the time, thought, and sacrifice to become who you desire to be.

WHAT'S YOUR PASSION?

That's right, today we're going to talk about passion. As in, do you have a juicy, fiery, get-you-up-in-the-morning personal passion, or, like most of us, a dusty one in the attic somewhere, that we used to love to do, back in 1982 ...?

For me, I have always aspired to be a writer. Some people are born with a silver spoon; I came with a Bic pen and yellow legal pad. Throughout childhood I surrounded myself with stacks of books and papers, scribbling notes for the always future best-selling novel.

Inspired at age twelve, I proudly wrote my first novel "My Mom and Me," the quality of which immediately brings to mind Anne Lammott's sentiments in *Bird by Bird*:

"Every writer has a book that will never be published ... This will be yours."

However, that writing attempt prompted my subsequent five-star poem on Paul Revere's Ride that actually made it to the principal's desk. My teacher proudly told me that the principal couldn't believe it was done by a sixth grader. At last, I thought, I have *talent*.

In high school I developed my writing passion through advertising competitions, earned national honors of all things, and wrote to compensate for obvious non-talents. Of note, when our college housing group did a classical music recital, I was without classical talent. Not wanting to be left on the sidelines, I composed and sang (using the verb loosely) humorous verse to the tune of Beethoven's 5th Symphony, a funny song that I still use in my speaking.

The important point here is that discovering and pursuing a passion is often not some climb-the-mountain shazammy experience—it's usually found in doing a little bit here and a little bit there. The trick is to level extreme thinking, which may seem like an oxymoron when combined with the word passion. Throughout my life I have kept writing, bit by bit, even when it's lousy, and even though I couldn't do it full-time.

And pursuing a personal passion has benefited our children, whether they realize it or not. We observe their interests and inch them forward. Of course, this depends on the interest—for example, if it's an airsoft gun passion, we largely ignore it. Our oldest son has had many passions (should I say obsessions?), starting with Thomas the Tank Engine, through Legos, adding Pokémon cards and finally striking gold with a coin collection; *this* we can get behind. We take him to coin stores (once a month tempers the obsession), find mentors (patient older neighbor coin collectors) and ask our friends to bring home coins from their foreign trips.

Maybe you're saying, "Super, but how do I find my own passion?" Begin with doing what you love. What fueled my writing was simply reading. As a child I soaked up all kinds of books, from Nancy Drew to *Lord of the Rings* (and didn't understand a word). Reading *Little*

Women, I identified with Jo—ink on my middle finger and our homemade version of the *Pickwick Papers*. Then in college I read the core classics: Dickens, Hemingway, and *People* magazine. All these deposits added to the passion account.

Whatever your interests—oil painting, pottery, or gardening—you can do something today: a summer class, supplies, an informative chat with an expert.

Developing a passion makes life's experiences more purposeful and fulfilling. Writing columns pre- and post-childbirth has helped me do personal therapy, share life-changing principles, and become a better writer. Instead of putting my pen and paper in a closet for twenty years, I now use our family life adventures as food for thought, helping others springboard to their learning along the way.

I invite you to rekindle a former hobby or discover a new passion for fun, and see where your positive passion takes you!

DREAMS COME TRUE, EVEN IF INCONVENIENTLY

My husband and I just returned from a trip to New York City. This was not your average trip. Not because I was seven months pregnant, mind you, or that we had our two eldest sons babysitting the rest of the children (bite the fingernails), or that I'd never been to NYC before.

No, what set this trip apart was that it fulfilled a personal dream of several years, and for several reasons. Besides wanting to visit one of the most celebrated cities in the world, and yearning to see fabulous Broadway theatre, the main reason was that one of my work-in-progress novels is partially set there. Yes, it's possible to write solely from imagination and research. But as my novel unfolded, my soul kept feeling, "Wouldn't it be great to BE there, to really feel the city?"

For the past few years I'd actively planned to travel there with my husband, but with six children something always seemed to trump it. And then the thoughts would begin, *Well, it's not really necessary,* and *it seems kind of pricey for a writing habit,* and *maybe it won't work at this stage of life.*

However, last year I came very close to the dream. I'd gotten my husband on board, even finagled it with his work schedule, and all promised to become a reality. On the very day I had finished making arrangements and only needed to begin purchasing, I left my computer for do a few errands. Upon returning, I quickly checked my email and found out that I'd been invited to speak at a large women's conference. In HAWAII. And guess when it was scheduled? That's right, the very same weekend I'd planned for us to go to New York. So we went for Hawaii (I know, hard to shed a tear), and put off the dream yet again.

So at the start of this year, I once again taped the picture of the Statue of Liberty on my Life Board, and this time told my husband the novel was almost done and I needed real-time research. Translation: WE. ARE. GOING.

And then I got pregnant. With our little caboose.

Of course I was thrilled about the baby, but at the same time I saw the NYC dream fading yet again. Then a few months later, a friend of mine spontaneously took a Christmas trip to Paris with her hubby, for a whole week, and had a memory-making experience.

That was it. I told my husband that NYC was *my* Christmas Wish and began researching travel plans again. Yes, I would have a belly most large. Yes, it would be in February instead of the ideal June. But doggone it, we were doing it.

And we finally did!

I have to tell you, IT WAS AS GREAT AS I HOPED IT WOULD BE. To finally go and feel the energy and pulse of the city, to hear the honking from taxis, and feel the magnitude of the soaring skyscrapers was beyond compare. Savoring incredible Italian food, standing atop the majestic Empire State Building, feeling small beneath the flashing NYC Jumbotrons, and taking in "Wicked" from great seats, the scope and feel of the city hooked me from the start.

As I returned to my novel, the thoughts, ideas, and descriptions became more alive, and with details to make it real (Dean & Deluca almond croissants!)

So I'm here to say, believe in your dreams. Keep setting those once-a-week goals. Because you truly never know when the opportunity will arise to fulfill and experience them. Keep planning. Keep progressing, one simple goal at a time, connecting it to your personal life vision.

On our return I shared with my children my appreciation for them and their father helping me make this dream come true. Then I showed them the Statue of Liberty picture on my Life Board that represented it. Now they can clearly see that if their big-bellied mama, ready to have her seventh, can achieve a dream, then they can achieve their dreams too, at any age or stage.

BEING A WOMAN, WIFE, AND MOTHER —AND SOMETHING ELSE!

I recently had the pleasure of going to lunch with authors Jennifer Nielsen and Rachelle Christensen. Both are talented writers with national agents. As we spoke about balancing our dreams with being a woman, wife, and mother, here are a few things we shared and agreed on.

1. *Create your core and stick to it.* We were delighted but not surprised to discover that our cores were the same—first God, then family, then dreams. What was amazing is that each of us had held to that core, and over the years our opportunities had grown. As Jennifer said, "Make your bargain with God." Tell Him your desires then commit to your part of it to keep first what matters most. As mothers, we can often do both—family and dreams—but we'll be fulfilled only as long as we put it in the right sequence.

2. *Go for the big dream.* Jennifer encouraged us to not hold back unnecessarily but go for the one we really wanted. As she spoke, I realized I had held back on a particular dream because I couldn't automatically see a way to do it that worked with my family. But an idea came to me that would not only work but be a blessing to our children. That's the beauty of talking with good women (and over good food).

3. Allow your family to be a part of it. Like most women, I've tried to pre-empt any negative impact from what I do on my family time. Translation: early hours, late hours, hurrying to finish before they get home. And while I stand by this, I've also learned over the years to let my family help. To let them be in the mix, hands in the thick of it, kneading the dough and helping it rise, so to speak. Instead of worrying about inconveniencing my kids or spouse, I've had to learn to let them be a part of it, as a memory maker, and we ultimately share the triumphs and tragedies together. Whether it's been hauling book boxes into a conference, delivering flyers on the four-wheeler, or exchanging money at a book signing, my children are learning life skills.

Case in point: after my teenage daughter recently spoke to a large group, many people came up to me after and remarked, "She had such a presence. She commanded the audience." She is thirteen. Though confident in her own right, I believe that her accompanying me on speaking assignments has increased her poise and speaking abilities.

So don't keep your dream and your family in separate universes--include everyone in the thrill of the adventure and you'll find that 1 + 1 = 5,235.

4. Be flexible. As I've made and used my Life Boards over the years, I'm constantly amazed how my dreams are achieved, but often in a different way than I had planned. Like my goal to do radio. For a few years I hosted an award-winning online radio show that reached fifty-two countries. Then I hosted a three-hour show for Bonneville Communications in downtown Salt Lake City. And I've also recorded radio podcasts right in my own home in my workout clothes. Each way has allowed radio to easily fit into family life during various seasons.

So don't merely create your Life Plan, but use it, involve your family, and enjoy the journey!

INVOLVE OTHERS
IN CREATING YOUR IDEAL LIFE

Sometimes our focus on self-improvement and goal setting makes us pull into our own little world, feeling it's all on us to succeed.

Not so.

A big—and fulfilling—part of achieving personal goals is to involve others. That's the true joy: allowing others to help you become, and in the process, you reciprocate the same.

Through my life coaching program, I've hosted online challenges to help women tidy up their lives physically, emotionally, spiritually, etc. One challenge participant, Carol R., shared a time when she had set a goal to weed her front yard. So far so good. But you know what happened, right? Immediately, there was an uncontrolled and unexpected change in the plan. However, Carol adjusted beautifully. She said:

"I wasn't sure I would be able to accomplish this goal this week because my daughter got strep throat, so I watched her kids for the week. That may not seem like a big deal, but she homeschools both kids so I had to homeschool too! I LOVED it but my time was pretty crunched. Then I thought, why not have the kids help me for an activity? They loved it and boy does it look nice!"

Fabulous! Carol involved her grandchildren and not only accomplished what needed to be done, but had MORE fun doing it while connecting with them, and teaching some life skills along the way. Does it get any better?

So remember, be your bold self and invite others to get involved in your goal adventure. And if they say no, no worries. Ask someone else, or try it a different way. It's creativity that finds the right solution.

No woman is an island, so enjoy inviting others to join you on the adventurous ride of creating your ideal life. You'll not only be more fulfilled, but they'll catch the joy of it, and perhaps invite you to join their ride too!

WOMAN

GOALS FOR THE JOURNEY

THE POWER OF CHANGE

As I began lifting weights the day after Christmas, and was excited to do it (both of which are no small miracle), I thought of how my life had changed over the past few years. That's when I remembered my "Year of the Change" many, many moons ago.

I wasn't in a happy place that year—physically, emotionally or mentally. In a quiet moment, I asked myself three life-changing questions: What isn't working? What do I want to do differently? How can I make it happen?

I realized the most significant goal I could set would be weight loss and energy gain (mainly, because I wore homemaker mumus and would wheeze going up and down our stairs). Using simple time-tested principles and a home gym, I did just that, becoming a trim small size full of life and energy. That change dominoed into the relationship with my husband. I stopped helping (nagging?) him with our growing business and let him do the honors, then focused more fully on my family and growing our marriage. Lastly, I began speaking a little here and a little there, sharing with women the concepts I had learned, which gave me confidence and fulfillment as I watched their lives change for the better, too.

Interestingly, from that one pivotal change my entire life blossomed. Things that frustrated me before were not only manageable but enjoyable. And currently, from marriage to children to helping women and families, I'm still reaping the benefits of that amazing year.

Is this your year to truly make a life change? Whether it's weight loss, finances, relationships, or any other thing, I invite you to answer those three questions above, and see how they can begin helping you create your ideal life.

To do so, you may need to step back for a minute. Sometimes we can be so hyper-focused on what is before and surrounding us, that we lose the big picture. We feel hopeless, without energy, and our thoughts turn negative when we dwell on things that irritate or anger us, instead of seeing life as a whole.

One woman I life coached was moved to tears, feeling frustrated with her marriage, her lack of progress in using her talents and abilities, and a lack of joy and happiness in her life. As we first talked through some key issues such as her physical health, and personal emotional and spiritual wells, she veered off into discussing her husband. Several times throughout the call as she veered in that direction I gently reminded her we were not discussing her husband's challenges, but rather what she could change and how to make that happen.

In doing this, I encouraged her to create her own Life Plan, including a paragraph detailing her ideal life, and then to choose one area of focus for her goals. I then encouraged her to create a Life Board—a space, poster board, or foam board—where she could post her goals, quotes, and pictures of her ideal life.

I received an email shortly afterward. This sweet woman shared that life had become so good that she hesitated even to create the Life Board because she could hardly handle the positive that was coming her way! Yes, she will have unexpected challenges to face as she moves forward in creating and living her ideal life. But now she has focus, direction, and hope.

When you really think about it, our present is also our future, and it's up to us to choose it. No matter your circumstances, and I've seen a few, you CAN truly change and succeed in ways you could not have understood before. Sit down for twenty minutes and answer the three questions above. Focus fully on your answers, making sure that they are from the gut and the heart. Then post it somewhere you will see frequently, allowing it to simmer daily in your heart, mind, and soul.

An anonymous quotation reads, "If not now, when? If not me, then who?" Make this your Year of the Change and live the joy.

LIVING A BEAUTIFUL LIFE!

I had to laugh the other day when the topic for my KSL TV Studio 5 segment was "Living a Beautiful Life."

I woke up that same morning to a daughter suddenly throwing up (a rarity), a son's allergic reaction to a wasp sting from the night before (I quickly made a sling), and my car not starting (it never does that). As my son and I tried every jumper cable we could find, my TV deadline pressed nerve-rackingly close.

My generally secluded neighbor tried her hand, but with no luck. Ultimately, my husband rescued me in the eleventh hour, though I was too late for my original segment slot and had to go on later in the show.

Ironically, as I drove downtown and verbally reviewed what I wanted to say, Miss America style, I got to the part of, "Living a beautiful life to me means feeling joy in the daily experiences" and burst out laughing.

Right.

However, as I considered the morning, I saw some very joyful things, one of them being the surprising and enjoyable opportunity for me and my neighbor to connect. Unexpectedly, we laughed, problem-solved, even shared experiences of the past when things had gone awry, the whole nine yards. It really was the best part of my morning.

Remember that the most joyful and beautiful moments often come in the thick of stress. If we will look for them, we will find them. Which is why living a more beautiful life on a daily basis is more important than waiting for that one special moment a year to satisfy. Here are some tips for living a more beautiful life, daily, in three core areas (Self, Relationships, and Life Skills).

For "Self":

*Purchase special just-for-you indulgences and slowly enjoy them as such. Instead of scarfing down half a bag of Oreos, I buy handcrafted lemon cookies, so rich you can only eat one or two at a time, savored best at night right after a bath!

*Light a candle by your bed as you wind down from the evening.

*Give personal gifts from the heart. One of my dear friends handwrote a small quote book for me, including favorite thoughts and sayings. Twenty years later, it's one of my most treasured possessions.

For "Relationships":

*Create an "Occasions" Journal, nothing over the top, jotting some fun experiences from the holidays. We wrote one year that our daughter checked to see if the mashed potatoes were hot enough by sticking her finger into the white mound. They were definitely hot enough, so much so that she burnt her finger. Now, for fun, we will hold up our finger and say, "Chelsea, are the potatoes hot?"

*Make an occasion out of the humdrum. I don't know how it happened but we began doing a French Toast Feast on Saturdays. We use thick-sliced toaster bread then add blueberries, raspberries, real whipped cream, and genuine maple syrup. Instead of lunch, now it's a feast. It's become an unexpected and tasty tradition.

For "Life Skills":

*When doing chores with your children, once in a while shake things up with something new. One day we cleaned the garage with the dangling carrot of a picnic and ice cream afterward. Nothing fancy but the kids were ecstatic and got the garage cleaned lickety-split (for a banana split...).

*If you have teenagers, do something out of the ordinary. Maybe order pizza for them and their friends, or buy some karaoke CDs. Bring out the plastic leis and cheap hula skirts. They can always safely roll their eyes and say, "Yeah, this was my mom's idea."

These are a few quick ideas for putting the "fun" in "functional." Yes, monotony is part of life. But when we add a candle here, an indulgent treat there, a spontaneous picnic or a random fun theme, suddenly life is beautiful.

BYE-BYE RESOLUTIONS—
MAKE LIFE CHANGES THAT LAST!

Making a life change is more than saying, "I want to lose twenty pounds" or "I will finish that novel!" It's knowing what you want, setting realistic goals, and rewarding your fabulous efforts.

Set goals from a Life Paragraph. Years ago friends gave us a plant for a hospitality gift. Having a decided Black Thumb, I determined to keep this one alive. I watered it diligently for two weeks until one day I looked at the plant closely and experienced an epiphany: it was a fake plant.

Oh, yes.

Flimsy one-time resolutions are like watering a fake plant—they aren't real. Successful goals come from connecting them to a bigger picture—your ideal life. Choose the ideal outcome you want first then use goals as vehicles to get there.

In order to focus your journey, create a Life Paragraph. It's so easy, but the result is powerful. Life coaching guru Brian Tracy has said, "The establishment of a clear, central purpose or goal in life is the starting point of all success." Once you have a clear paragraph of what you want from life, goals are easier to choose and achieve.

To create a Life Paragraph, brainstorm buzz words to describe your ideal life in three categories: Self,

Relationships, and Life Skills. For example, in Self you might have, "positive, spiritually centered, emotionally healthy, fit," etc. After brainstorming all three areas, combine and edit them to create one juicy paragraph, about six to eight sentences long, which captures your ideal life. Have fun with this! Tweak it until you feel it best describes what you'll work toward.

Real goals for Real People. Good goals are specific and make you stretch, but not feel so overwhelmed that you down a cheesecake. I've coached women for ten years, and my secret to their success is one goal a week. That's it. Choose wisely and then go to it. Motivational speaker Hyrum W. Smith wisely suggests including the following when writing your goal: make it realistic, timely, specific, measurable, and action-oriented. Translation: "I will write 3,000 words this week during three, 1-hour sessions from 9 to 10 p.m." Or, "I will do a FUN workout three times this week for twenty minutes, varying cardio and weights." Voila.

As you set goals, be flexible, and you might find something better. One of my writing goals was to finish a novel I'd worked on for a year. But, another plot idea entered my mind, accompanied by entire scenes already playing out in my imagination. I focused on the latter and finished the rough of *Caribbean Crossroads* in just over sixty hours. And, I returned to my previous novel refreshed and better prepared.

You can't believe what you can achieve by combining your Life Paragraph with a well-chosen goal— only one—each week. I've been able to write and publish books, be a public speaker, be a stellar mother to seven children (that's up for debate), run our home generally well (except weeks before, during, or after holidays), and enjoy it (most of the time). All while not being particularly special or tremendously talented.

Reward Yourself and Keep Going. After setting a goal, choose a reward and use it! One woman paid herself five dollars for each work out then put that money toward a new outfit. Go girl! Rewards help change your neuro-associations to goal-setting—a fancy word for salivating Pavlovian style to set and achieve a goal, all because of the promise of an hour-long nap. At least, that's my kind of reward. Whatever you choose— go on a cruise, buy a new outfit—use it to keep yourself focused and committed.

So create that Life Paragraph, choose a connected goal that motivates you, and reward your efforts along the way. This is your year to create fabulous change, so go get it!

GET ORGANIZED LIKE REAL WOMEN

If you hate getting organized, stop trying to be Martha Stewart, and instead try one of these quick tips to jumpstart change.

1. **Accept some chaos.** Understand that no matter how many great tips or fabulous formulas you use, if you have a family, there will be mess. It doesn't mean you have to accept it everywhere, but simply not to stress when the garage is untidy AGAIN (not that this happens at our house, every other week). Or that your children don't remember their dishwasher day AGAIN (every Monday and Tuesday). Or that the boys' bathroom continually smells like, well, a boys' bathroom (again and again and again...)

2. **Bite off chewable chunks.** You don't need endless hours to complete a task, but you do have to be content with a little here, a little there. A few weeks ago my goal was to declutter the kitchen cabinets. So I did one drawer, A DAY. Can someone say excruciating? But that's all I could do with my baby, my other six kids' schedules, and my online life coaching program. But it's paid off. Tonight, at the last minute, the kids wanted to make s'mores, and in a moment I was able to quickly say, "The crackers are up above the fridge, the candy bars and marshmallows are in the kids' cabinet, and the metal skewers are in the bottom specialty drawer." Can someone say Stellar Mother Moment (that no one appreciated but me)?

3. **Stop making so many lists.** I could probably start a support group on this. My BFF is generally a large sticky pad in a bright color. Very sad. So a few months ago I had an epiphany—stop rewriting the same things and like Nike, just do them. So I did. I made one list for the week then went through it daily. When something new needed to be added, I opted first to just do it. It was utterly amazing how many of the "yucky" things (i.e., filing, sorting, tracking) I got done that usually got bumped to the next week's list.

This works for quick cleaning too. One day I noticed that the silverware tray was full of crumbs. I went to write it down, then realized that it would take me almost as long to empty the silverware, wipe out the tray, and put it back in. Within minutes it was done and I avoided an additional "to do" pulsating in the background. So next time you're tempted to write something down, ask yourself—can it be done now?

Remember, getting organized isn't about white-knuckling your way through several months of work, and then breathing a sigh of relief. It's changing a little here, a little there, and making it work for you.

FEEL THE FEAR … AND BABY STEP

I had been invited to speak at a rather large event. Of course, to me, anything over two people is considered large, but this was in all respects a rather large event. The invitation came as no surprise because I had pursued it and been excited about it right to my earlobes. Until I got a phone call from the event manager asking for my book and talk CD (what, a book? A CD?), which needed to be delivered to them by a very early, out-of-the-question date.

I stared into the phone, looking for an answer, or mercy, and suddenly I had lockjaw. I hung up thinking words from an 80s song—"At first I was afraid, [then] I was petrified." How could something I'd desired to do for so long suddenly paralyze every facial muscle I had at the thought of doing it?

For a full half hour I sat frozen with fear while my kids climbed over me like a human jungle gym. Thankfully, my husband eventually came home from work. And as I gently shared with him my dilemma—as in shook his shoulders and wailed "HELP MEEEEE" or something like that—he gave me the best bit of advice of our entire marriage. He said he had had a similar experience that morning when he had put the chimney caps on our home. The roof is very high (measurements don't compute with me so I will say it compared roughly to the Notre Dame cathedral). And this he-man, tool-man, contractor-to-the-core felt fear. Hunkering down by the chimney, he sat for a minute, when the thought came, "Focus on what's in front of you—don't look at the ground." And so he did. The entire time he dangled from the precipice he simply focused on the chimney cap. It was a cinch.

As I listened to him I had my own "aha" moment, the click of "that is exactly what I needed." I took out a sheet of paper and listed a few small things that could get the ball rolling: as in, "wake up." As in, bathe, feed and love my children, and then breathe. And later, when the kids napped, make two phone calls and go sit at the computer. Just sit.

This may sound a tad underachieving, but it worked. The same thing happened to me when I was doing an exercise program (let me dust the cobwebs off that memory) and I had made a goal to work out three days a week. It was a Wednesday morning, the day assigned to begin being a size four. And then the alarm went off. As I lay there thinking of many excuses, some of them quite good, a thought came to mind: "GET yourself out of bed, down to that bench and sit there until you get something done." (Important point: success began with the choice to just sit.)

Next time you face a project that strikes fear in your heart, focus on what's in front of you. Make a short list of lame-o things like "sit in a comfy chair for five minutes with pen and paper." The rest will come because the mental paralysis is lifted by already accomplishing your goal.

Wise words from *What About Bob?* come to mind: "Baby steps." Take those baby steps, focusing in front of you, and go baby, go.

FOCUS YOUR ENERGY, THEN LET IT GO

Do you get through a day and feel like you've been spinning your wheels? Can I tell you that my life has been like that in great measure this week BECAUSE MY BABY WILL NOT SLEEP AND I CAN'T GET A BLESSED THING DONE.

Did I mention this is causing me stress??

Because so much of our daily society is wrapped in busyness, we tend to start strong and laser-beamed on Monday, only to find we've been putting out fires through Friday instead of focusing on what matters most.

In *Good to Great*, a fabulous book by Jim Collins, he discusses what makes good companies into great companies. One concept he shared was about the flywheel—that as a company focuses on one major concept and turns the wheel (no matter how long it takes to make that one turn), they should continue to turn the wheel until it creates its own momentum. Then the wheel will take off in flight with hardly any effort.

I find the same thing for my time and energy. As you go through your week, remember the concept of one juicy goal per week. This keeps your focus on exactly what will move you forward in the thing that absolutely matters most to you. When I lose sight of that and get mired in the 56th post-it note to myself, I realize that not much is getting accomplished. I'm spending my precious energy on avoiding what is vital and feeling overwhelmed about the whole thing.

If you do this, stop and ask yourself, "What is the most needful thing this week? This day? This minute?"

On one particular day I had been fretting about what to share for this particular column. Since I wasn't getting anything urgent accomplished, I went with the rhythm of the day, spending a good portion of it playing with my children (WHO WERE NOT SLEEPING, did I mention?)

Sitting outside in a chair, I enjoyed the beautiful fall day (cheering my kids' bike riding from a chair can be considered playing). But still, I had to be productive. So I brought out my fifty-seventh post-it note, breathed a heavy sigh and said, "What is the most needful thing to get done today?" And as I thought about it—though there are 257 things that could have been chosen—I honestly could not think of anything more pressing than to write this column. Such a simple thought made it suddenly seem doable. And everything else sort of melted away.

Miraculously, at the same moment my baby became sleepy and went down for a nap. My older children came home from school, gave me loves and quick info, then snacks and off to build a fort. Unbelievably and unexpectedly, I ended up with this time to myself, uninterrupted, with an easy flow of "Hey Mom" from my little ones while I typed the column.

All was right with the world.

So the point is to focus your energy on the needful thing. As you do, everything else melts away for a moment in time, including your stress, and opens the door to doing.

WOMAN

CREATE HEALTHY CONNECTIONS
ON THE JOURNEY

KEEP IT SIMPLE

The other day I was engaged in the very serious negotiations of ... a carpool. Yes, it was that time of year when grown women make a mountain out of a molehill, taking something that is seemingly easy, and making it infinitely more complex, simply because we can.

It began when a friend e-mailed that her child would be attending the same school, to which I replied, "FABULOUS–CARPOOL!!" But this then evolved into a five-family ordeal that involved schedules, rotating seating assignments, allergy restrictions, and headlight checks. Not really, but it was headed there.

So we involved another person.

After talking with the first lady, I conversed with the second one, sharing what I wanted and laying out our options. Then she used this most wonderful, electric phrase that changed the dynamic of our conversation. She said, "Well, what works for me is ..."

Shazam. That hit me like lightning, the perfect confident-woman phrase. No emotional hysterics, no whining, no hidden meanings to decode behind self-sacrificing speeches and smiles. Wow. She briefly stated what worked for her, which ironically was what worked for me. Easy, flexible, two days a week, and no stress.

Ahhhhh.

Was it supposed to be that simple? I felt a sudden loss of sorts. There had been no emotional trauma, no three weeks of going back and forth and someone being offended, then the necessity of bringing the olive branch fruitcake. It was done in three minutes. And then we moved on.

When arranging similar nightmares in your own life, remember this one thing: keep it simple. Do not let being Room Mother consume your life to the point that it requires more plans than a wedding reception. And do not feel guilty when it is two weeks into September and your child has not signed up for a single activity.

Enjoy this week by looking at commitments, car pools, work assignments, special projects, and whatever else is on your plate, and ask, "How simple can we keep this?"

ALL I REALLY NEEDED TO KNOW ABOUT COMMUNICATION, I LEARNED FROM MY COMPUTER

Two things you must know about communication: First, I love my journal. Call it narcissistic indulgence, kid sanctuary, and/or cheap therapy bundled in one. Over the years, countless typing hours have been dedicated to my life epistles, recorded from age ten.

Second, I do not love my computer. Instead, we have an understanding: I push the button—it comes on. I type, I save, I push the button—it goes off. If it took out the garbage with the same dependability, my husband would be in trouble.

For eight years this understanding worked perfectly. Until I upgraded. Like something from *Knot's Landing*, the computer dumped the old journals for a newer program, and I was the last to know. Gone. Two hours of typing, every Sunday, for eight years, thousands of pages of my life, obliterated. Perhaps this is an appropriate place to discuss good communication skills, namely how to express yourself effectively. On a good day this means to validate, set your stakes, and get closure.

To validate means to empathize; I did empathize with the computer man—for about five seconds. I reigned in the PG phrases and instead validated his feelings; meaning, listening first and then expressing that I understood. For example: "I understand you may have told me I would lose all computer memory in an upgrade, I just don't remember." Gary and Joy Lundberg, authors of *I Don't Have to Make Everything All Better*, believe that validation is essential to good communication. In this case, it is finding positive common ground, something honest that says, *I do think you're a good person, even when I want to rip out your tonsils.*

Next, set your stakes. Let the listener know your clear expectations, beginning with "I need." Referring to my negative computer experience, perhaps something like, "I need this resolved; I don't care what it costs or what you have to do." (Additional threatening facial expressions are optional but not recommended.)

Lastly, get closure. Or their business license. Do this by saying, "I will," keeping control over what you can control—yourself. "I will call tomorrow to see what you have found." Adding, "thanks for your time" or "thanks for talking with me" is helpful, but not always possible.

These three principles—to validate, set your stakes and get closure—are all you really need to know about effectively expressing your feelings; and although they will not retrieve lost computer data, they will improve your communication skills.

LOSE EMOTIONAL WEIGHT AND GAIN NEW ENERGY!

Women deal daily with emotional burdens that can bring us low and drain our mojo. Try losing one of these behaviors, and gain instant energy.

Feeling Less Than. Too often women waste energy comparing themselves to the next gal— how successful her children are, how clean her home is, how skinny she looks two weeks after having a baby. But when we stop comparing, we experience more life contentment. Years ago we moved into a home in the woods, away from suburbia and fishbowl living. Finally, we had a place our noisy children could play and run free. The land was gorgeous and the house average, but a larger home was not our focus.

Then an acquaintance stopped by "to see the new house." From her comments and expressions she made it clear that this house was not what she imagined for me, and not "as good" as what we had come from. And suddenly I felt "less than." But a wonderful thing happened, and hopefully this idea will help you too. When I went back to what I knew (which was that we'd bought the house to help our family be happier, not to impress her or any other would-be visitor), I felt my contentment return.

Forgive. Anger and resentment—even when justified—suppress our natural joy and motivation to live, love, and do. So in the end, we only rob ourselves, clinging to this heavy load that becomes an obstacle to our joy. But forgiving isn't about being unwise. If someone has done something horrible to you and obviously has not changed, you don't go asking for trouble. But you can give the gift of a Clean Slate for the past, a Get Out of Emotional Jail Free card, which will ultimately be most freeing to you.

Recently while listening to a talk, the thought hit me unexpectedly that I hadn't forgiven someone. Though I thought I had, after examining my behaviors I could see a thread of holding the hurts over that person—not consciously, but emotionally—by not fully letting them go. That night I decided to give the gift of a Clean Slate. I focused on changing my responses the very next day and saw an immediate change in myself and the other person.

Find your unique self and share it. Too often women lose a sense of self, then become resentful that their family only sees them as the errand do-er or the go-to-gal. If you want to do something enjoyable or expresses yourself but don't know how, if you don't have energy or don't know what to do, start with who you are and what you love.

I began writing fiction on the side—hideous stories devoid of proper grammar or solid plot lines. But as I aged and continued to write, my stories improved. Eventually, I wrote and published my first real fiction, a clean romance titled *Caribbean Crossroads*. I was completely shocked when it was nominated for a writing award, and later hit number one on an Amazon

Bestseller list. Who knew? So whether it's knitting beanies for babies or sharing recipes with tofu, do something that uniquely shares your wonderful self. Let go of fear of failure or embarrassment to try.

Get rid of the emotional weight that's holding down, whether it's a grudge or a fear or something in between. And enjoy the fresh new energy you gain!

ARE YOU A PEOPLE PLEASER?

Over the past few months I have been feeling lack of motivation, surges of frustration, and plain fed-up-ness. But I've been unable to put my finger on why. This weekend I finally realized one of the main reasons for these emotional waves: people pleasing.

Unwittingly, I had begun doing some things to be helpful in different areas of people's lives and had now become entrenched in their needs, situations, and perceptions (i.e., "I have an emergency and you are my rescuer"). It began to dawn on me, again (how many times do I have to learn this?), that I had become the nearest option to a solution.

So I talked with my hubby about that on Sunday and felt closer to resolve—you know, we women have to verbalize before anything starts moving.

By Monday the final fed-up point hit, and I said, "I am done." That morning I made a firm resolution to restore balance and stop being the yes-woman.

Not ten minutes later I received a call from a really good friend, asking me to babysit, for a really good reason. I said no. Kindly, calmly, I explained what I was doing. Then ten minutes later I took my daughter to preschool and a lovely woman who never asks me to do anything, said, "Can you babysit for me tomorrow?"

Isn't this how it is, as soon as you determine to do it differently? Again, I kindly and calmly said no, but did explain briefly what I was doing. Before you know it, she shared being in a similar situation, and that she had now become the go-to person in areas of others' lives. We both left the conversation, I believe, inspired and empowered to no longer say yes when yes was not the wise thing to say.

So, I invite you to go back to balanced. Look at your life and ask, Are my absolutes suffering? If your family needs you more right now, then say so. If you can't take on another service project, then say so. It may be time for you to pass the baton for a season.

If someone asks you to do something, simply say, "Let me think about that," or "Let me check our family calendar first." It's wonderful to know people can rely on you, and can ask for your help. But pause before answering them and simply evaluate what is vital for you and your family right now. It may be a time for you to step back and let others step forward.

I will enjoy this next little while of getting back to center, nabbing it before it gets too out of control. And I will savor lying down for ten minutes before my baby wakes up. That's something I can say yes to.

HAVE YOU EXPERIENCED
THE POWER OF AN ARK?

The other day my mom shared an experience that got me thinking about the power of an ARK—an "Evan Almighty"-ism for an Act of Random Kindness.

My mother was standing in line at a thrift store and overheard a conversation between a humbly dressed mother and her young daughter. As her daughter approached her mother excitedly clutching a pretty "party" dress, her expression quickly faded as she heard her mother say, "We can't afford it."

It cost $10.

My mom stepped in at that point and explained that her granddaughters regrettably didn't live close by, and that she would be thrilled if this mother would allow her to pay for the dress. It turned out that it was the young girl's birthday.

Another friend shared an encounter her mother and sister had experienced. As coupon queens, they had finished their shopping, purchasing about $1000 worth of groceries for about $30. As they exited the store, thrilled by the rewards for their hard work, my friend's mom noticed a man sitting in his car eating a pudding. Something struck her as odd so she walked over to him, started a conversation, and found out he that had fallen on hard times. Having just scored with their coupons, the two women gave him three full bags of groceries. Before leaving the gentleman explained to them he had taken a paper route to help make some money, and would they like one of his extra Sunday papers to say thank you? When the women got home, these coupon gals found out that the paper contained not the usual one coupon section (which you're lucky to find), but FOUR coupon sections.

I love these experiences. Within our family, we've received many ARKs this past year with the new baby, from friends babysitting my other children to my mom temporarily taking over the laundry (ah, the joy of folded kitchen cloths). Symbolic of this service was a neighbor who brought our family dinner. But it wasn't merely dinner—she had made a huge pan of incredible fajitas, with all possible delicious sides, in pretty disposable containers to eliminate dish duty. And a huge dessert (note: three happy teenage boys). And the cutest outfit for our new baby (note: three squealing girls). And a Body Shop bath kit to rejuvenate a tired mama (note: one ecstatic woman). The time, energy, and thoughtfulness that went into this ARK made me feel overwhelmingly loved, and full of desire to do the same for someone else.

In each of these situations, a person's life was made brighter and their step a little lighter because someone noticed them, understood their situation, and did something to make it better.

Enjoy this week finding your own ARKs, both giving and receiving, without fear or embarrassment.

DEALING WITH
EMOTIONAL SEPARATION

In C.S. Lewis's classic tale *The Great Divorce*, a story about the divorce of Heaven and Hell, Lewis describes the journey of a person taking a bus trip to visit Heaven. As this person asks his guide why such a large downtown as Hell has so few people living there, the guide replies, "The trouble is that they're so quarrelsome. As soon as anyone arrives he settles in some street. Before he's been there twenty-four hours he quarrels with his neighbor. Before the week is over he's quarreled so badly that he decides to move ... But even if he stays ... {he's} sure to have another quarrel pretty soon and then he'll move on again ..."

And so it is in modern day. How many times have you heard, felt, or said, "I can't deal with this anymore, let's just move." We live in communities and drive on the same roads with the nonverbal understanding that we are each doing our best. But living side by side, we are open, vulnerable, and over time will inevitably experience situations both difficult and delightful. When things get difficult, it is easy for us to react defensively and look questioningly at the neighbors we thought we knew. When something goes sour—from the non-returned weed eater to a character slander—we feel hurt and instinctively pull away.

But in these times one thing stands true: What is important in this life is that we love. Such love for everyday people like ourselves can be complex, a constant push-pull of our soul, testing our strongest feelings of justice and mercy, right and wrong, and the ability to still love somewhere in between.

This is not pretending that we didn't see it, feel it, or know it. It's looking beyond what we see, feel, and know to a fuller understanding, believing that every person is trying their best to get up, breathe, and face the day. And for many, even that can be a Herculean task.

In his book *Illusions*, Richard Bach reminds us that the people in our lives are there for a reason; what we choose to do with them is up to us. We can pull away, and for a time that may be necessary. But our soul knows that, in the end, true happiness is found in learning how to stay connected in the face of emotional separation.

Religious leader Neal A. Maxwell taught that we are here to learn how to partake of the bitter cup without becoming bitter. Loving while hurting is one of the hardest things we can do. But pain is a powerful teacher if we let it be, and as we seek for deeper insights from a higher source, we can find the purpose in it.

If you are experiencing an emotional challenge, try to look at it another way. Take a time out in a different place, mentally or physically, and look at the situation with an open viewfinder, without blame. As you desire and ask for peace you will see it, feel it and know it.

71

One lady recently said, "People are human, get over it." But do more than that. Don't avoid it. Go through it, be a part of it. Perceiving and embracing people as people, with all the wonderful, weird and wounding things we do, helps us to embrace those things within ourselves.

WIFE

MEN AND WOMEN:
APPRECIATE THE DIFFERENCES

MY DEGREE IN GENDER EDUCATION

In college, I learned fascinating truths about behavioral differences between men and women, but not from a class. It came from walking up a tall hill on a frosty morning with my dress tucked in the back of my pantyhose. Happily unaware, I remember thinking as I walked along, chirping and cooing to the young man I had casually caught up to, that it was unusually chilly that morning. I even wished I had worn a long coat instead of a short jacket. I remember the great number of students, both in front and behind us, all heading for our eight o'clock classes.

And upon first reaching his class building, I lastly remember, after saying a coy good-bye and turning to go, his voice flatly echoing across the morning campus, "Hey Connie, your skirt." This was when I swept my hand behind my lower half and found, well, my lower half.

I spent the next hour in class not thinking on the elements of biology, but on the rudiments of human behavior, two to be brief (no pun intended). First, why, during my twenty-minute death march, didn't anyone tell me about my unintentional exposé? And second, why was the fated messenger a man?

When a guy has a zipper down, men do not nervously hesitate then discreetly take him aside and whisper "X-Y-Z." They say, "Dude, your fly's open," and go about their business—with no lingering shame at having noticed and no need to apologize and tell another friend about the embarrassing incident. How many women walking up that hill had, in sheer terror, watched me sway in the wind, and yet were unable to tap me on the shoulder and say, "X-Y-your whole backside."

As I sat in class, I became confused about the ways of a woman. (And by the way, that roar you hear is the loud, agreeing applause of men nationwide.) This is a gender who can categorically pick lint balls off a stranger's suit coat or tuck exposed dress tags (with an accompanying shoulder pat to say, "Now you're dressed"), but cannot tell someone their dress is stuck in their nylons.

Your college tax dollars finally paid off that morning as I experienced my educational epiphany—this feminine duality can occur because the latter (dress in nylons) is confrontational, carries too great an unknown, and is just plain embarrassing: What if I offend the person? What if she gets mad? What if she doesn't like me and then two months later I see her in the grocery store?

As you can see, there is too much at stake. With lint, we are safe because we are socially justified. No court of law would convict us for picking off a lint ball, or for that matter a loosely flying hair, because that's what you do with a lint ball or a loosely flying hair. It's that simple.

For those of you still confused (another roar), the behavioral bottom line is this: When interference is emotionally pricey—e.g. trailing toilet paper—a woman will stick to the weather and the color of your shirt. Class over, see you next week.

THE FOREIGNER

Men have a difficult, if not impossible, job of translating the female language. This takes an inordinate amount of time, energy, and discovery. And although fluency in another foreign language is not necessary, it does help. My husband majored in Japanese and I believe this has been a great benefit to our relationship.

What makes speaking to women such an adventure is that every syllable, every nuance, is a dramatic part of the conversation. The words, alas, are somewhat of a nuisance. It's the pitch, the tone, the inflection that makes the conversation a true masterpiece. For example:

Superficial Chat Voice: "Did you get your daughter into the Einstein Preschool?" (Translation: Mine got in and I couldn't be happier and want you to ask me all about how to nominate me for Mother of the Year.)

Take No Prisoners with a Superficial Chat Voice Response: "No, I didn't. It wasn't what we wanted for Veronica." (Translation: What? Registration can't be full already, it's two years out! How will I get her in? How did you get yours in? How will I be nominated for Mother of the Year?)

Print cannot do justice to a woman's range of emotional voices, a spectrum that makes the color wheel look monochromatic. My children are fine tuned to these ever-so-slight intonations. They understand that when I say with a half-whine, "Please get in the car," they

76

have time for one more Popsicle because they know I will repeat this phrase with increasing intonations, going from annoyance to severity to exasperation. Physical movement only occurs when I reach the threatening eyebrow and tight-lipped, "Get-in-the-car-now" moment.

The differences in male/female ranges come into wondrous view when meeting an acquaintance. When a man sees a dear friend (referred to simply as a guy), they both look in opposite directions or move invisible objects on the ground with their toes. Although they never make eye contact, they carry on a complete conversation and at the end feel completely fulfilled (or rather, not the slightest bit aware of fulfillment because they couldn't care less).

When I see a dear friend, the high-pitched noise brings dogs for half a mile. "How ARE you, you look SO GOOD!!!! Did you get your hair lightened? Really, it is so natural!!!" This is one complete sentence, makes complete sense and after the conversation we both leave feeling we have in some way just attended an operetta.

Ultimately, this attempt at the complete conversation experience is what makes communication such a lifelong adventure. To women I say, live the range, and enjoy expressing your emotions. To men, I offer my condolences.

A TALE OF TWO GENDERS

I had my own terrible, horrible, no good, very bad day and talked to a friend about it. As I broke down in emotional waves over a pint of Ben and Jerry's, my friend listened intently, nodding in understanding, and responding with "You're kidding," and "I would have told them to eat rocks," and other appropriate phrases. Obviously, this was a conversation with a woman.

Later, when I related the same incident to my husband I got, "Really," "Really," and an all-out "Hmmmm." The sooner women understand that men will never communicate like our girlfriends, no matter how sensitive and validating they may be, the sooner we will appreciate our spouses (and how patient and verbal our girlfriends are).

Appreciating communication differences is not so hard. We need to be clear about what we desire and how it can be fulfilled, without always looking to our husbands to fulfill it. Translation: figure out what you need. This can be a challenge because my needs change about every 24 seconds, negating what I barely told my husband yesterday about what I really need from him.

For example, yesterday I told him, "But what I really need you to do is ask me what's wrong." However today, at 3:42 P.M., he is asking repeatedly what is wrong and it is annoying. I say, "Stop asking me what's wrong—what I really need is for you to hold me." You see where this is going. I don't want a husband, I want a psychic.

Remember, both men and women are working with their best understanding, with the tools at their disposal. I read that a man is emotionally 25 years behind and although I don't put stock in this, it is food for thought.

Vice versa, it is said a woman experiences a hormonal swing every thirty-eight minutes (or was it thirty-eight seconds, or thirty-eight swings . . .). He knows that when I break down sobbing over a twisted vacuum belt, there are some things he will never understand about the female gender.

When a man and woman share communication needs, it makes connecting more effective. Try asking your partner one thing that would aid communication for him or her; e.g. a pause, an eyeball, a blink. Learning each other's bottom line leads to more effective listening, expressing and even, hopefully, enlightenment.

I experienced one such "light-bulb moment" after worrying I was unintentionally aggravating my husband because of my chattiness. When I asked him what he thought about this, he honestly replied that he loved to hear me talk; it helped put him to sleep.

JOY IN THE DIFFERENCES

I had an experience recently that reminded me how beautiful it is that men and women are different.

Every year my husband and I make a goal—OK, I make the goal for my husband—to have a monthly personal interview with each of our children. A few weeks ago on a beautiful and relaxing Sunday morning, I casually brought this up (Rule #1: The more casual the request, the more likely it will be heeded), and he said, "That sounds great. In fact, I will do it today."

Wow. With my enthusiasm bubbling over, I took my first unwise step toward the dreaded Overzealous Wife. While my little ones slept, I ran upstairs and made a "Stellar Sokol Family" binder, complete with tabs for each child's name. I typed thought-provoking, insightful and validating questions with answer spaces that my husband could fill out along the way. And what sheet of validating questions would be complete without a weekly goal and, of course, a reward description... followed by their choice of sticker?

Are you hurling yet?

Oblivious to my over-achieving ways, I bounced down the stairs in search of my husband. He emerged from the boys' room with the news that he had completed his interview with our youngest son. WHAAATTT? Without the new Sokol family binder with personalized tabs?

After I sheepishly showed him the binder, he smiled and shared how the last hour had gone. First, he had researched a few excellent resources that had suggestions on child interviews. One talk had related a story about when he interviewed his daughter. It was formal, dry, and completely boring. But he soon wised up and instead, began going for ice cream and chatting to get the scoops (no pun intended). After that, whenever the dad asked for an interview, his daughter would say, "Dry or wet?"

My husband told me that he and our son had had a blast, talking, wrestling, and eating a snack while he got said scoops.

To both our credit (and I mean *both*), we laughed about the binder and I reassured him that it wasn't vital to use it (of course, my mind and heart were trying to align on that one). But it did show me once again how differently men and women do things AND THAT IS OKAY.

If, like me, you struggle with this, then seeing the beauty in the difference is crucial. Everything in life doesn't have to be structured with a check mark. Sometimes I feel we as women overlook the very real and very needed benefit of a husband's spontaneous personality. It will usually drive us mad to a certain degree, but overall, it keeps life juicy and us from taking ourselves—and child interviews—too seriously.

This week, enjoy relaxing the structure and allow your husband's endearing, last-minute, shoot-from-the-hip ways to more fully influence family life. If you usually run things on a tight schedule, choose one thing you can be more casual about. I'm not talking about things that are value-based or vital, but things like letting children have some down time on a Saturday morning if they would usually start right off with chores. Or—if you're like me and are the Bedtime Nazi—let them stay up to watch a family show once in a while, like we did the other night with popcorn and "Ben Hur," all eight of us on our big sleigh bed.

Enjoy that things are done differently. Find the humor and the benefit in doing things a new way and you might find yourself having fun!

PASS THE POPCORN, HONEY!

While reading a national magazine, I was struck by one particular article on doing nothing. The writer shared that her husband, a journalist, knew how to procrastinate with style. That sleeping, watching TV, eating, and generally being good to himself were all part of the creative process. And that after giving needed time for an idea to develop, the piece would spill forth and practically write itself.

Often I think we women are not as bugged by our husbands as we are by their ability to be unaffected by our "bugged-ness." We marvel at their ability to be lazy, to mindlessly click the remote while the overflowing laundry basket sits at their feet, and not feel one bit badly. Perhaps we are bugged because we can't shut it off; we can't stop our compulsive behavior or sit still without guilt.

I remember reading in an article that sometimes we fulfill our responsibility not by acting but by doing nothing. So ask yourself, "Is it crucial?" If not, then instead of seething at the kitchen sink, muttering that you're not the family slave and that on your wedding day you were declared a wife not a Merry Maid, go sit with him. Leave the dishes and go slide onto his lap, hold the popcorn (or better yet, bring some), and ask who's winning. Not that it matters. He could say Smokey the Bear, you could say great, and the conversation would be considered a success for all involved. What matters is to occasionally give up the agenda.

Follow the adage "if you can't beat 'em, join 'em" (or the equally effective: if you can't cajole/threaten/ bribe/instill gut-wrenching guilt, give up and get ice cream). Release the I-must-get-this-done-now list and change it to the It-can-wait, It-wasn't-that-crucial, or if you must, the How-can-we-share-this-lame-menial-chore list.

Sometimes it is important, but just as often, you can ask yourself a second question: who is it important *to*? If your husband, your son, your neighbor always needs something done, and you feel you haven't time to sit down or go to the bathroom, then ask, "Who is this important to?" If Bobby needs a shirt pressed, RIGHT NOW, because he has to go, RIGHT NOW, then perhaps Bobby can learn how to turn on the iron, RIGHT NOW. If it's important to Bobby, he will iron the shirt. The sooner Bobby releases the unrealistic but common expectation that you be the Mom-On-Call-Ironing-Serf, the sooner Bobby will begin to truly appreciate, in that moment of panic, the generous offer from Mom-the-Awesome-Timely-Shirt-Presser.

Ask yourself these two questions: Who is it important to? And, is it crucial right now? And perhaps spouses everywhere can spend more quality time cuddling in loving arms than avoiding cold shoulders. And remember, to truly do nothing together, one must *do nothing*. If those around you don't understand this, happily remind them it's part of the creative process.

HEROIC HUSBANDS DOING THE DAILY DOS— *THAT'S* SUPER POWERS

With Superman, Spiderman, and every other comic-book-gone-movie that's on the silver screen as of late, I've thought a lot about what makes a man a super hero. Know what I've realized? It's possessing the super power of being a good husband and father.

For example, my husband recently raced home from a stressful workday, scarfed down a quick meal, and carted six children to a seasonal corn maze. There, instead of engaging in the frightening fun, he held hands with our young daughters, diving into the corn kernels (and later shaking them from his shoes), encouraging them on a bull ride, and going with them down a slide. He could have been relaxing with a remote but was instead cheering on a pig race and taking turns holding our baby while doing it. Thoughtfully, he brought me roasted pecans, lugged the diaper bag, and in a manly yet tender way dressed our baby in a fuzzy-bear winter outfit to ward off the chill. Observing all he did—quietly and without fanfare—I felt overwhelmed with love for him. He could have been doing anything else, anywhere else, but he wanted to be with us.

How often do our good, loyal husbands do the everyday thing, when what they really want is to go four-wheeling? Or eat a hot meal without interruption? Or not help a pouting child with math, or an obstinate tweener with a science fair project? How many men look longingly at a powerful sports car while driving a dying minivan? I think about my husband's new truck—not brand new but a solid buy. Its tailgate was stolen a few months after purchasing it, and our new-driver son accidentally scratched the paint down the entire left hand side.

Sometimes women think, "Nobody understands what I go through in a given day." But our husbands do. Even if they don't verbalize it, they experience it. Often, they don't complain about it much, realizing that tomorrow, there will likely be more of it.

So this is my shout out to all good, kind, hardworking husbands everywhere. Thank you. Thank you for loving your families, putting food on the table, and setting up Scout tents year after year in all kinds of weather. Thank you for changing the oil and hanging the Christmas lights, for showing a son how to man up, and for apologizing when you let him down. Thank you for being real super heroes with real super powers. The world truly needs you now more than ever.

Ironically, while walking down a grocery store aisle and thinking about whether this topic would be right for a post, I saw a living example of my subject matter— a dad in a holiday Superman suit, price checking on Aisle Seven. Decision made.

Here's to Heroic Husbands.

WIFE

MEET EACH OTHER'S DIFFERENT NEEDS

HE NEEDS/SHE NEEDS

While my husband gave me an impromptu shoulder massage after a busy kid-filled day, we stumbled on a parent/child correlation: marriage could be defined by diapers, meaning she wants Pampers and he wants Luvs.

While working on my muscles, my husband concluded that basically, a woman wants to be pampered—for her husband to allow her to let down, to be soft and vulnerable and tenderly loved. I surmised that a man needs luvs, to feel his wife's adoration, to connect with her as woman and wife, and to know that he is the most important thing in her life. As cheesy as it may seem to either, we agreed that when both parties' needs are fulfilled, marriage is a bit of heaven.

But reality check—how does this happen? One couple I know shared this experience: the husband returned home one day and saw from the permanent marker on the wainscot and her relating the toy marble extraction from their toddler's nose, that his wife had had a difficult day.

He then asked her, "Where are you going tonight?" She limply replied, "I did the grocery shopping this morning so I won't need to ..."

"No," he said, "where are you going tonight, honey?"

And she understood. Suddenly visions of Rest, Relaxation, and Rocky Road filled her tired soul. In those moments, words cannot communicate how a wife feels about her husband, how his understanding softens life's edges and fulfills her needs.

Conversely, when a husband walks in the door late from work, *again*, and meets She-Bear-With-A-Threatening-Frying-Pan, he knows luvs will not be forthcoming and wonders if dinner will be set on the table or thrown on his lap.

But when a man is greeted with all the warmth, confidence and gratitude that only a loving wife can best bestow, he is renewed. His natural state is enhanced and he is more than he was before. Suddenly, he can change diapers.

If this rings true for your marriage, perhaps once this week, when you hear his car in the driveway, grab lipstick and perfume. Greet him at the door, just you, with a three-second kiss, and then ask him meaningfully, "How was your day, honey?" (Do this before he walks in the door and sees cereal for dinner.) He will know you love him.

By knowing, communicating, and fulfilling each other's needs, by Pamper-ing and Luv-ing each other freely, marriage truly becomes a joy.

NURTURING VERSUS COEXISTING

Years ago when my husband was severely ill, I went back to work for a short period of time. He watched our eighteen-month-old and tried to recover his energy, while I typed for eight hours in a small cubicle, in a dungeon-like warehouse room, surrounded by countless other dismal cubicles. From that work experience, besides understanding the definition of hades, I noticed something I hadn't before: I needed a happy, nurturing wife.

Because, you see, I would get up, dress and feed our baby, then hurry out the door to work at that gray, dreary place, taking only fifteen to twenty minutes for lunch (mostly because I couldn't take the downer atmosphere that also pervaded the gray, dreary employee lunch room). Then exhausted, I would hurry home, fight traffic, worry about my husband's health and son's well-being, then ready myself for some respite and nourishment, only to arrive home and find—Phase II.

Phase II was walking in the door, hugging my son and husband, assessing the situation and what needed to be done, and starting all over again. Fixing dinner, tidying the baby mess, cleaning the bathroom, and folding the laundry. By bedtime, I felt like a hot bath, which I didn't have the energy to take, and crying myself to sleep.

The good news is this: I truly came to know how vital, how absolutely nourishing it is for a husband to return home from a horrible day of slaying dragons, to find a happy wife with a hot meal on the table, and a somewhat tidy home. It's not a throwback to 50s culture or female enslavement—it's pure heaven.

Gary Chapman, author of *The Five Love Languages*, shares this thought: "Married adults long to feel affection and love from their spouses...That kind of love begins with an attitude—a way of thinking...that says, 'I am married to you, and I choose to look out for your interests.' When your spouse's emotional love tank is full, the whole world looks bright."

So this is my invitation to nurture your spouse. I like to put toothpaste on my husband's toothbrush at night, which he knows means, I love you. Or I buy him wool socks at Costco to see him get downright giddy. Or when he comes home from work, I fix a fresh dinner plate for him while he greets the children and puts away his work items. Although these small acts may seem inconsequential, these nurturing moments become the mortar which cements the big bricks of daily married life. These moments make a spouse feel that while we're building something meaningful (the relationship), we're enjoying the process (the fun).

Perhaps today you can make his favorite dessert—the messy kind that you tend to avoid. Or rub his back while you watch a show together—ten minutes will do. Or write a short card that says, I appreciate how hard you work and all you do to balance work and family life. Whatever you do, each attempt to nurture your spouse replaces coexisting to create a warm, fulfilling marriage.

THE ONE THING MEN WISH
WIVES KNEW, BUT CAN'T TELL

In Shaunti Feldhahn's book *For Women Only*, the author posed the title as a question in a national survey of 400 Christian men, ages twenty-one to seventy-five. They could have said anything, and did—hoping for more understanding, respect, sex, and effort from his wife to take care of herself. But even when a man could finally have the ultimate say, the number one thing he wished his wife knew was this: how much he loved her.

That this concern was double the percentage over any other response, I was amazed. Though men had real concerns, this was their biggest. If a similar survey were given to women, I'm guessing it would have been a laundry list of "You shoulds" fighting for the number one spot. So what can we do to show our husbands a little bit of the same Christian heart? Maybe taking a look at the lower items on the survey is a good place to start.

Make an effort to look your best. The sheer work that keeping up with children requires, never mind with the effects of having borne them, can sometimes cause us to unwisely conclude, "Well, we're married so he'll just have to deal with it." Yes, our husbands love us, but they're men, and what says love to them is trying to look our best. And no need to be a Victoria Secret model.

One man said, "We need to see that you care about keeping our attention on you—and off other women. It helps if I see my wife purposefully working toward staying in shape." Note, working *toward*. None of the men felt a woman had to be a skinny-minny. If a woman did her hair and makeup, she often looked confident and comfortable in her own skin. This made the husband feel proud to be with her.

Understand his major conflict: Men struggle with the constant tug-of-war of wanting to provide for their family, but spend more time with their wives. As women it can be difficult to appreciate the daily struggle this is for a man. As one surveyor said, "I feel confused. You want me home more, yet you want a new house, nice things, income, etc. I feel like I am pushing two big rocks uphill." It's similar to how you may feel, wanting to look good but to also bear and raise children—it's a give and take.

The more we can comfort, appreciate, and specifically thank our spouse, the more empowered he'll be to approach this dilemma with greater desire and creativity, rather than feeling guilty and resentful. Over the years I've written cards to my husband thanking him for all he did to balance the "rocks." One day I noticed he had kept those cards in his office, and this is a man who doesn't keep much. This said volumes to me about how much that validation had meant to him.

Make yourself available for intimacy. This can often be the most difficult for us as overworked and overtired mothers. But for men, physical intimacy equals love, a physical and emotional need. To put it in simple terms, imagine being told to go without chocolate—for days, weeks, even months—when you really, really need it. So this week, try making yourself more available and let him know you love him in the way he needs to feel it.

Consider what you would have put in that survey—the one thing you wish your husband knew. I know I have, and upon reflection I've realized that the men had it right: having my husband know how loved he is really does trump all.

HOBBIES AND PASSIONS:
YOURS, MINE, AND OURS

As a professional speaker, I welcome the opportunity to talk with women about their lives. One consistent thread in our conversations is about pursuing personal hobbies. Surprisingly, questions inevitably arise such as, Are we allowed to? How often can we do them? What about supporting his hobbies and pursuits?

Being married doesn't mean chained at the hip. It does mean creating connecting experiences together, whether that is found in doing hobbies you like, he likes, or hobbies that you can enjoy together.

Over the years I've seen how key it is for the wife to jumpstart these connective pursuits. For example, I wanted to visit downtown New York for writing research and for pleasure. I could have done this with friends, my writing group, or my daughter's dance troupe. Instead, I invited my husband to share my world. So together we traveled to New York, and he became part of, not apart from, my writing dream. In that chilly February air, we experienced that fabulous city, including going to the Seagram building where part of my novel takes place. Now when we watch *A Family Man* and see the same building, we smile and share a connection.

But connection through shared hobbies doesn't always have a storybook ending. After realizing one year that my husband was in a work rut, I signed us up for scuba diving classes. Freezing in the public pool, stopping off for an appetizer at a chic bistro, fearing for our lives at forty feet below in a mountain crater, these experiences—although some less than perfect—created bonding moments between us.

At the end of class, I chose not to complete the certification (read: traumatic forty-foot mountain crater dive). My choice didn't ruin the experience, however. On a future scuba diving trip, we both knew that he could make the dive and I could read a book (or, in his version, I could prepare a gourmet meal and be ready to massage his back when he returned topside.)

Even when interests differ, we can still support each other in them. My husband loves to golf, and I heartily encourage him to: he relaxes and returns ready to be with the family. And as our children have grown, he has taught them how to golf, too. Now, a favorite part of his golfing hobby is taking our three sons.

This kind of support is reciprocal. Every year my husband gets me the same birthday gift—a writing overnighter—and I love it. For twenty-four hours, I can spread out my writing notes without them being trampled. I order room service, then type to my heart's content, without interruption. Talk about a win-win—he doesn't stress about what gift to get, and I anticipate the unchanging, upcoming joy.

As a couple, consider ways to support each other's individual hobbies already pursued. And decide on a new hobby you both could enjoy, possibly one that doesn't require scuba diving in mountainous craters.

ENCOURAGE EACH OTHER IN EVERYDAY LIFE

As a wife, and especially a mother, life is moving at warp speed. By the time you finish dinner, homework, bathing children, family time, and tidying up, you're either in a coma or it's morning again.

Not much time left to cuddle, connect, or support each other in lifelong aspirations.

However, carving out such time can make the difference between life feeling moot and mundane, or motivational and marvelous. Finding out what makes your spouse happiest in life, and asking how you can help increase that, definitely improves marital relations.

Discover one dream or goal of your spouse. Maybe it's to take down a twelve-point buck. Or hike K2. Or sing karaoke for the Fourth of July reunion. Whatever it may be, listen, learn, and let him know you want to help. Ask what ways you can be supportive. Your spouse may not need your help, but they will generally appreciate encouragement. So when that happy hunting trip comes around for him—and perhaps that annoyed feeling of being left out for you—this time you can wave good-bye with a smile and a joyful heart. Mostly because you'll be working on your dream/goal while he's gone. And don't be surprised if he's more likely to support your dream/goal when he gets back.

Ask one thing you can do to show love. Just one thing. And for a specified time period (this week, month, etc.) For example, the other day I asked my husband to tell me one thing he'd like me to do for him during this upcoming year (a dangerous question to be sure, right after, "How do I look in this swimsuit?") Wisely, he took time to think it over before he answered. He could have chosen anything—perhaps a spotless home, freshly ironed clothes, or an uninterrupted football game more than once a year. In the end, he opted for my help with special meal preparation due to his recent health issues. With this one choice, he felt loved, I felt relieved (anything but freshly ironed clothes), and ultimately, our relationship will be blessed.

Use a gentle conversation starter. If you're feeling less than overwhelming support from your man as you strive for your own goals, consider giving a soft reminder. Saying things such as, "I had a great experience with my writing group this week," or "Can I share with you what I learned at my painting class?" can give helpful nudges. These conversation prompts may feel juvenile, but often husbands don't think like a woman (spoiler alert). Men appreciate gentle prompts to remind them what their wives want to talk about (which generally does not include the Steelers or HEMI engines).

Follow up occasionally with questions like, "How's that dream/goal going for you?" "Anything new with (your dream/goal)?" or "Great job on (dream/goal)— what's next for you?" These kinds of questions, genuinely asked, make a big difference in how loved a spouse feels. And surprisingly, he might remember to ask you in return.

As you find out each other's lifelong desires, and kindly remind one another to talk about them, you'll find a spark return to your relationship.

That's a great goal.

THE POWER OF FORGIVENESS

I believe the most startling aspect of forgiveness is first discovering that you need to practice it.

Years ago, a wonderful person spoke in a meeting about the power of forgiving our spouse. I listened with self-contented ease. My emotional slate seemed clean, and so all was well. Then a feeling-thought came to me: You haven't forgiven him. Instinctively, I silently replied, Au contraire. I have forgiven him. For many things. Repeatedly.

But as I let the words sit in my soul, I realized the feeling-thought was right. We had both come from dysfunctional homes and had sorted through our share of baggage to finally create a strong marriage. But in a corner of my heart I still held back, and held over him a feeling of distrust and disrespect.

The solution to the situation came just as clearly—a gratitude journal. That very night I found a small, empty notebook in my desk and immediately wrote an entry. From that day forward, this journal has enabled me to continually focus on my love and appreciation for such a good husband. Letting go of the past and moving on has helped me not only be and feel more grateful for his love, compassion, and willingness to do things differently, but has ultimately changed my life.

And it's changed his. After that meeting, something fundamental shifted within me that I never verbalized, but which he must have felt. Because that very next day his responses to me also changed. Without saying a word, we both became more kind and patient with one another.

Author M.J. Ryan shares, "By opening our hearts to the people and things that challenge us, we become spiritually and emotionally supple. [These people and things] become interesting opportunities for further growth, rather than threatening obstacle courses we must endure. From this place, we actually can enjoy life more, whatever is happening."

Changes in people generally happen slowly, line upon line, experience upon experience. But sometimes, it occurs suddenly, even abruptly. Regardless of the timetable, change brings us closer to truly loving, and becoming.

Ultimately, what matters most with forgiveness is that we attempt it. After we take that first and often most-difficult step, asking humbly, "What's my part?" we then become aware. We see our participation in the problem, and then can own and change our behaviors and mistakes. When we act on that new knowledge, we gain greater clarity—not only about that specific situation, but regarding life itself. As we continue in this softening cycle, changes unfold in ourselves and others.

That's the power of forgiveness.

FILL YOUR SPOUSE'S BUCKET, WATCH YOURS OVERFLOW

We all know speaking positively is powerful. But do we realize how powerful it is in marriage?

Renowned marital therapist Dr. John Gottman teamed up with mathematicians to record the number of positive and negative interactions between married couples during a fifteen-minute conversation. If the ratio was 5 to 1 for the positive, or near it, they predicted the couple would stay together.

Ten years later they had correctly predicted who divorced and who didn't with 94 percent accuracy. And from only a fifteen-minute conversation.

Is speaking positively to your partner important? It's absolutely key. And it doesn't need to be in a sugar-sweet, "Pollyanna" tone, either. Positive interactions are as simple as saying, "Thanks for picking up those grapes for me" (even if they are the wrong color), or "Sweetheart, would you mind taking out the trash this morning?" (Instead of, "Did you forget the dang trash, again?")

And as is so often the case, treating others well benefits us, too. Eliminating the negative from our lives not only brings greater life fulfillment, but avoids the mental and physical damage caused by stress, anger, and hostility. Positivity helps us recover faster from pain and illness, and even leads to an increased life span. A study by the Mayo Clinic showed that negative people cut off more years from their life expectancy than if they smoked cigarettes!

One prominent researcher, Barbara Fredrickson, added that being positive broadens our thinking, builds durable physical and emotional reserves, improves overall performance in a group, and can transform people mentally and emotionally.

So if you're wishing your spouse would change, consider shifting your own positive to negative ratio. For today, listen to your words. Mark a planner, paper, or even your hand each time you say something kind. At the day's end, evaluate not only what you can do better, but ask your spouse ways they like to be praised. Small and simple things can create the greatest and deepest of changes. As you think and speak more positively, one thing is certain—a change is guaranteed.

WIFE

TWO DIFFERENT PEOPLE BECOMING ONE

LOVE IS LIKE A LEAKY FAUCET

I know that for many of us, marriage can be like a perpetually leaky faucet. *Why does it always leak?* you ask. *Why can't I fix it? Or, I thought we fixed it last week—why is it leaking again?* Then we go to a plumber to get it fixed, a very expensive, educated plumber. But when it springs another leak, then it's the plumber's fault. And what kind of a plumber is he anyway?

The bottom line is that at some point all of us have bad plumbing, an unplanned leak or things we can't seem to fix, no matter what duct tape we are trying. To deal with marital leaks, here are two suggestions (that can also be obtained from an educated plumber)—find the source and find the humor.

Finding the source means asking the question, is it habitual or replaceable? Don't worry about determining which is which, because they are the same—depending on perspective and choice of you and your significant other. Habitual can be anything repetitive, from scratching a beard to coming home late, and these can be replaceable but only if the "offender" chooses. If the offender is the "significant other," this can be significantly frustrating and feel as if you have no control.

Happily, you do have control over you, and therefore can choose a response, and make it replaceable or newly habitual. If your habitual response has been frustration, complaint or sarcasm, you can replace it with a declaration of your feelings and some good self-care. This means to calmly share how you feel, then go take a hot, bubble bath. Regularly. Or enjoy a good book, or a very large cheesecake.

Then move to step two, finding the humor. Surprisingly, this step gets easier when you use a code word which works as an automatic tension diffuser. When my husband becomes distracted in our conversation, I say, "Eyeballs." This conjures a vision of my little preschoolers who, when I require their attention and say "I need your eyeballs," pretend to graphically gouge their eyes out and throw them at me. Or when my husband is going on about the barge rafter not melding with the ridge beam, and he apparently doesn't notice that he lost me back at the rebar installation, I will say, "My father was a piano mover, so ..." Instead of being irked, we smile and are entertained. Mostly.

Next time you are confronted with a marital leak, try finding the source and finding the humor—and voila, instant duct tape.

WORKING WITH A SPOUSE'S TIMELINE

In marriage, each spouse becomes aware, responds, and grows at a different emotional rate and way. Knowing a few coping skills in marriage can help you endure, embrace, and even enjoy your spouse's marital-growth timeline.

1. **Take the long-term view.** Sometimes in relationships we women get frustrated with the apparent lack of short-term progress. Focusing on the long-term outcome keeps our perspective. Remember that with personal change it generally takes thirty days to create a new habit, and six months to a year to create lasting change. But don't forget the many years it first takes to create awareness, then change neural pathways to start and keep the change.

The good news is that research shows men are becoming more emotionally intelligent husbands, with about thirty-five percent of them better understanding, connecting with, and being influenced by their wives. So things are changing. It's just a little slower than some may like. However, I've noticed at the park, mall, or movie theater at least fifty percent of the time men are the ones handling the babies or small children. Years ago, that was not the case.

2. **Make reasonable requests.** Reasonable requests are about assessing a need, then discussing and doing something to fulfill it.

For example, years ago I had four children, six and under, so I approached my hubby about taking a night out for myself. He said, "Why do you need a night out?"

Hmm.

So after an enlightening discussion he came to understand that the *need* was not negotiable—I needed time to myself before I went AWOL. The compromise was on *how* it happened. We opted for me taking Wednesday nights at Barnes and Noble with a good book and a slice of cheesecake, after which I came home a new woman, wife, and mother. This was a reasonable request—a need to be filled—and we found a healthy way to fill it.

When trying to make this kind of reasonable request work, don't go to extremes. Avoid the attitude of "I'm doing it and too bad for you," or the martyr-like, "I guess it's not possible." Instead, state your reasonable request, then offer a few possible solutions. In this instance I could have proposed trading babysitting with a neighbor, or a different night of the week, or early Saturday morning. What matters is that the need is validated and the compromises attempted. If your husband doesn't quite understand, choose a solution and give it a trial run for a few times, then both evaluate how it went.

3. **Create positive coping skills.** To ease the frustration of different timelines, develop a set of positive ways to deal with it. Connect with friends, work out, or create. Finding a personal hobby or interest is huge, especially for a woman. Even spending as little as fifteen minutes a day on your hobby can relieve stress,

boost self-esteem, creativity, passion, pleasure, accomplishments, and even decrease depression.

Throughout married life my hobbies have saved my sanity and brought me joy. Many years ago I began writing stories, lame to be sure, but I improved. Then I wrote for a small newspaper, then for a larger newspaper, then published a book, and now have several published books. Wisely using chewable chunks of time to write helped me complete the projects while bearing and raising seven children. And the process helped me not only be happier but to stop watching the proverbial "marital-growth pot" boil.

As you patiently work through marital changes, employ these three things and you'll feel more joy and peace while experiencing the natural timeline of marital development.

LET GO OF ANNOYING MARITAL CONTROL

I had a great learning experience this week over...corn.

We were hosting our annual big July 4th BBQ on Wednesday at our home. Having forgotten to pick up corn on the cob beforehand, I asked my hubby to do it on his way home from work.

As he got closer to home, he changed the plan to return home and shower *first*, then get the corn. Because I didn't know what time the corn stands packed up for the night, I began to feel the beginnings of I-must-have-corn-for-our-party anxiety. No corn?

Heaven forbid.

We went back out together to get the corn (not that I was supervising or anything), and as we got closer to the nearest city I saw the first stand completely empty, no one there. (Gasp)*There's not going to be corn? It's OK*, I reassured myself, talking in my head like I was doing personal therapy or something. *We really don't need it, it's all right, I should have remembered at the store.* I felt my heart thump, my blood pressure rise, and pretty much my whole world suddenly collapse because of the ABSENCE OF CORN.

My hubby said, "No worries, WE WILL FIND THE CORN!" and proceeded forward like John Smith in exploration.

That's when it hit me—*WHY AM I BEING SO RIDICULOUS ABOUT CORN ON THE COB?* Why was I making such a deal about this, making my husband feel like a failure and giving myself hives simply over a starchy vegetable?

So I turned to my hubster and apologized and said pretty much what I said in the above paragraph. He smiled, said no big deal, and right then we saw a corn stand *teeming* with corn as well as other goodies. And I had barely shouted out, "Oh yummy! Raspberries!" before my husband had bought and brought them over to the car for me to enjoy.

Ladies, we have good men. Sometimes they are annoying, even really annoying, but then so are we. This week I encourage you to chill out about sundry items like the weed whacker, the messy garage, and even—yes, I'm saying it—the all-important summer corn stand.

WHAT NOT TO DO
TO CHANGE YOUR MARRIAGE

At a large women's conference, I met a woman who talked about how to deal with her husband's ex-wife, affectionately termed "The Beast of Burden." At that same time, I was life coaching a woman who felt that her husband negated what she did, making her feel inferior and incapable, and at a loss about what to do. And another woman I was life coaching was trying to connect emotionally with her husband, but couldn't get past making it a task list.

How should we go about our attempt to create change in our marriage? Whether you want to jumpstart positive change or to wring your special someone's neck, marriage can be made more whole, in a lovely irony, by NOT doing a few things.

Stop focusing your energy on the other person. I know you hear this all the time but trust me, TRUST ME, I have been there, done that, and don't ever want to go back. Yes, his behaviors (or hers) are absolutely driving you mad, are excruciating to live with, and may be the nearest thing to an emotional black hole that you will experience, but FIRST, for a time, change your focus. Stop magnifying the negative so that it engulfs you; it only zaps the positive energy that could be used to create buffers, bucket-fillers, and a beautiful life.

Don't wait for permission to create change in yourself. Too often we wait for men to give us the signal that it's now our turn. Stop waiting. Or we may wait for him to make a change. Not likely. Recognize that you will have to ford this stream first, and to do so you will need a healthy focus of your own. Brainstorm things you like to do or things you have enjoyed in the past.

Too often women can't remember what it's like to go play hooky (not hockey) or get lost in a passion or hobby. Believe me, it will make you a nicer person to live with and actually helps buffer others' behaviors. Because you are filling your bucket with positives, and developing your own life (which women so deeply need on a consistent basis), you will be able to handle what comes with more confidence and peace.

Eliminate the negative emotion. This is probably one of the most difficult things to do. Do what you must to eliminate negative emotion. This isn't the same as stuffing feelings; that will only make you turn to a pan of brownies. This is about acknowledging that what someone did hurt you, deeply. Then journal those feelings, along with one or two ways you can handle that situation better next time.

For example, if a person is speaking rudely to you, you can smile and say, "I so appreciate when you speak kindly to me." If they persist, say firmly and kindly, "I will not be talked to that way. When you're ready to speak kindly, I would love to talk," then walk away. Do not stay to be dragged into a dead-end conversation.

This will take practice, but you can do it. Choosing one of these ways will make a great difference in the way you feel about yourself, never mind the other person.

Remember, stay focused on the Big Picture—what you eventually want. Time and tide are on your side. As you focus on the positive changes occurring in your life, it will get fabulously easier.

MARRIAGE IS LIKE A VIDEO COVER

My toddler son and I were casually lying on the floor doing carpet angels (snow angels on Berber) when he turned and smiled at me adoringly. Feeling a whoosh of warmth flood through me, I smiled back.

Then he smacked me with a video cover.

Promptly, with firmness, I said that was a no-no, an owie, a big ixnay. After his lip quivered momentarily, he once again smiled adoringly.

Then hit me with the same video cover.

It wasn't until later that I realized my two-year-old was teaching me something about marriage. There are many marital things that seem like continual smacks in the face. And change is often imperceptible, because marital improvement is a long-term process.

Every marriage has "video covers," issues that negatively affect the relationship and take a long time to improve. What's important is that the issue is not abusive, that the video cover is just a metaphor, and that you both—individually and then together—set boundaries of what is necessary to develop your particular relationship. Marriage is about incremental improvement, and the sooner we get used to bringing necessary issues to the kitchen table, so to speak, the sooner we can objectively understand how to grow our marriages. Not to mention enjoy them.

What kind of video-cover issues are affecting your relationship? Is it chronic tardiness? Dealing with unchecked anger? Perhaps it's unemployment, or being so busily employed that you both seem to be living parallel lives.

Choose one issue and decide on one thing you can personally do in your own life to alleviate the problem? Write it down somewhere, anywhere, and work on it to completion, which means until you feel a change in your life. When you focus on one issue and change one thing, you will see the difference in your life and consequently in the relationship.

To illustrate, consider hypothetical Betty and Bob's problem—he enjoys a ritual bedtime snack. The problem? Noise and location. It may have been pistachios or shelled peanuts, but after about fifteen minutes of crunching and flaking all over the bedcovers, he finished up with a hard-to-open plastic package of crunchy, crumbly graham crackers.

Out of the many solutions Betty considered (ear muffs, a Dirt Devil), she chose to read downstairs. Occasionally, she shared his noisy snack (with the understanding that his contribution to her resultant "love handles" means that he will love them). After a few such compromises, her husband unexpectedly offered to eat noisy snacks in the kitchen.

After the euphoria of discovering a solution you may say, aha, it is solved. And then you will get hit with the video cover again. This will create frustration—how many times do you have to get hit with the cover to know where this is going? But no one knows where it's going, truly. And the moment you say, "That's it, I can't take this one more second," something changes. Because you have either given up unnecessary control or set a necessary personal boundary.

Define the issue, change one variable, and see it to completion. And remove any video covers.

HOW TO STOP HOW-TO

After delivering my fourth child in six years, I felt a tad overwhelmed. My thoughtful hardwood-floor-installing husband offered to do household chores while I rested upstairs. First on the list (on any woman's list) was the Dreaded Linoleum Kitchen Floor. Mentally calculating the time needed for the remaining chores, I figured the floor should take him twenty minutes.

For those of you laughing at the time estimation, remember I was on painkillers. An hour and a half later I could stand it no longer. What was he doing, painting the Sistine Chapel? Bravely, I waddled to the top of the stairs where I saw him—pushing his large hardwood floor machine with buffer pad shuddering over the small linoleum floor. I was speechless.

Laura Doyle, author of *The Surrendered Wife*, believes that though women complain about their husbands' lack of assistance, they offer little relaxed opportunity for men to assist. "Many women are terrified that their husbands won't know how to perform everyday duties properly when left to their own devices." But leave them to their own devices we must, if we want truly loving relationships.

How to stop the ominous how-to? Today, notice how often you tell your husband or children how to—how to legitimately load the dishwasher, how to save ten minutes getting to the store, or how to map our chore schedules, and still have time to whittle. When you ask someone to load the dishwasher, do so and leave the room. Do not hover, supervise or suggest—simply leave it alone. Save for very young children, people unfortunately do not need our dishwasher expertise and will ask if absolutely necessary, or not.

Mrs. Doyle further suggests "stop telling your husband what to do, what to wear, what to say and how to do things, even if you think you're helping. As much as possible, mind your own business." For those unused to this, it will be difficult. You may experience tremors, anxiety, and the need to consume large amounts of chocolate. This is a withdrawal period and that's OK— once you're through this, you will emerge to a place called appropriate responsibility.

It is a wonderful place.

Suddenly you will be thanking family members for folded towels that look like bowling balls or mowed lawns akin to a NASCAR track. You will appreciate their efforts without criticism, without comparison. This does not mean you don't desire things to look, smell, or be nice. It means that you will think twice before you sacrifice the self-esteem of another person for a *Home and Garden* veneer.

Today, eliminate the unnecessary how-to. Instead, replace it with a good book, a phone call to a friend, or a few minutes to sit in a chair quietly, watching your son fold the bowling balls.

MOTHER

REACH FOR THE IDEAL

THERE'S A NEW MAN IN MY LIFE—
8 LBS., 15 OZ.!

Having spent the last nine months pregnant with our seventh child—at 46!—I'm feeling the new baby experience. But not just the physical. I'm experiencing the beauty of birth that I'd forgotten—the smell of a newborn, his soft skin, his sweet smiles and coos, his little hand resting confidently on my neck.

I wrote *Motherhood Matters* while pregnant, and I can honestly share after going through the birthing process yet again, I feel even more strongly—if that's possible—how true that simple phrase is. As I hold him, feed him, and care for him, a deep and connected love continues to wrap around the two of us, the kind of love that is hard to describe but that compels me stare at him for long periods of time without doing one single productive thing.

And not caring.

When I first found out I was pregnant, several worries went through my mind (important things like, how fat will I get?). But these quickly transitioned to more serious concerns, like chromosomal issues, our other children's responses, and the long-term effects on my older body. But I can honestly say that all the things I worried about have come to naught. Sweet Bryson is healthy, strong, and without any apparent issues. My children have not only taken to him but actually fight to

121

hold him. And if anything, I had more energy during my pregnancy than usual (is that possible?).

I've learned much through this experience already—a good deal about submission to things we are given and not necessarily seek—and about faith in God's timing. I continue to see how perfectly tailored this experience has been, and continues to be, for me and my family.

So I encourage you to embrace the difficult in your own life, knowing that even with the worries, concerns, and very real issues at stake—now and in the future—things have a way of working out, not perfectly, but as they should.

Now I must get back to my more important projects—nuzzling Bryson's neck and capturing his yawn on film.

A MOM'S SACRIFICES
FOR THE UNSEEN OLYMPIAN

As I recently witnessed the hilariously nervous reaction of U.S. gymnast Ali Raisman's parents as she competed in the 2012 U.S. Olympics, I found myself thinking that we parents are all the same. No, I'm not the parent of an Olympian, but I do feel what I do on a daily basis is pretty Herculean. Finding the lost swimsuit, overdue library book, or lost tooth—in the nick of time—is after all, fairly amazing stuff.

When I look at what I and other mothers do, day in and day out, I can see the building of an athlete, but not in the typical every-four-year sense. I have felt that same parental fear and sideline encouragement, not during a gymnastics meet but in their moral decisions or difficult life experiences. Like when they've needed self-control rather than engage in a school fight. Or were betrayed by a friend and had to work through the painful repair process. That nervous, "Come on, Ali—catch it, CATCH IT" was true for me, too.

Maybe it was because of my baby's recent birth, but during the Olympic London games it seemed that motherhood was continually being referred to, not as an interference, but an enhancement. Just ask Kerri Walsh-Jennings. This U.S. Olympic beach volleyball player, and gold-medalist, was asked if now being a mother to her two boys was a distraction at the games. Her fabulous answer was no; in fact, they were a help to her. They were part of the "team" and traveling together with her sister as a nanny, the family helped give her the strength and vitality to compete and win. Fulfilling that truth, she won another gold.

What I got from both the mothers competing and those cheering from the sidelines was that a mother's love makes the difference. That confidence and courage for and in her child gives an incredible gift unmatched by anything performance-enhancing.

In another interview, super poised teenage Olympic swimmer Missy Franklin shared that though she was approached by corporate sponsors with healthy financial offers, she declined them to remain an eligible swimmer for her high school team. Missy's parents also resisted pressure from well-meaning people who advised her to have their daughter leave the small-town environment and train elsewhere. Missy wisely shared that if she had done so, her swimming would have suffered because her environment of family, friends, and a trusted ten-year coach is precisely what made her successful. How does a seventeen-year-old get that kind of wisdom? Look at her parents.

As my family and I heard these stories, I couldn't help but feel a shared parental pride through this worldwide experience. My children are not future Olympians (unless there's an event for Dirty Socks on the Floor) but my everyday love, encouragement, and care gives them the strength to face competitions of the day, now and tomorrow. To be kind when someone is cruel; to be honest when it looks more lucrative to cheat; to put family first in a world that hesitates to trust in that truth.

Consider the countless ways you mother your children and prepare them for those white-knuckle moments of life. And give yourself your own gold medal, for being the right coach for them at the right time.

SOAK IT IN

Right before our annual Weekend for Women conference, life became very adventurous. Lots of fun little goodies happened (i.e. technical difficulties with printers, companies, printer companies, computers with printers, anyone or anything within a five-foot radius of a printer ...)

It had been quite busy and each day I had been trying valiantly to practice being mindful, balanced, calm, and not duct tape my active two-year-old to a chair. She cannot stay still in a diaper, bedroom, or fifty-foot enclosed space.

As I scurried to finish details and take care of loose ends, my baby awoke and it was time to get back to being the mama. At first, I have to admit, I was feeling bummed and pressured and wondering where I was going to get the time to be the mom and the other things too.

Then my son suggested we do a picnic outside, with sunshine and fresh air. Though I debated, thankfully, I agreed. On the spur of the moment, we slapped together some ham sandwiches, got chips and natural soda spritzers, grabbed a blanket, pillow and bubbles and went into our front yard.

What a gift!!

The sunshine warmed our backs as we munched on our "samiches," nibbled on chocolate-covered pretzels and listened to the first bees buzz around in the sky. My little ones rode bikes around the driveway, chased bubbles, gave me smooches and laughed with absolute carefree joy.

A great reminder for me, which I am sharing with you, is to remind us to SOAK IT IN! *Life*, that is. To stop doing the "essentials" and remember the "vitals." To pause, breathe, and know that as we let go of this driven, must-do feeling, we allow a higher power to take over the details and help make it happen. Seeing small miracles in our lives not only rightly humbles us, but gives us a beautifully deep and poignant gratitude that makes everything in life suddenly A-OK.

ARE WE HAVING FUN YET?

As much as I could complain (should I use that word?) about my sweetheart's creative ways of parenting, I wouldn't change them. Okay, maybe one or two things, nothing major. Sort of. But I'm learning about the benefits that his male perspective can bring.

On my way out the door for my Wednesday Night Out, I asked him to please keep the kids on a schedule, preferably the one used in our home. When I arrived home a few hours later, I was delighted to see the five-minute pick-up had been an apparent success.

"Wow," I said, "the place looks great, honey."

Stone-faced, but with a twinkle in his eye, he corrected, "We were cleaning up the *galaxy*."

Aha, the secret. As the night continued, I saw how this space theme got things done. When I asked if they had brushed their teeth, my son flashed his pearly whites and leaned in knowingly. "I had space bugs."

When I commented on my other son's neat Lego bracelet, he looked disgusted, "It's a *Buzz Light-Year laser*, Mom." Amidst the italics, I stood corrected. Harnessing their hyperspace energy, my husband accomplished what would have taken me more time and probably more chop-chop, let's-get-it-done mentality, and they had fun.

Are we having fun yet? Can we say today, last week, or last month that we have had fun with our parenting? One of the "funnest" summers I can remember so far is when my then two children, about three and one, had the Summer of Play. We literally played. Every day we went for a walk, sometimes two, pointing out trees, rocks, bugs, all the essentials. The kiddie pool was a staple, as was the after-swim smushy popsicles and warm towels. The local dollar theater showed quality kids' movies, and sometimes we splurged on movie meals, just because. Laying on the grass or telling stories at naptime, it was by far the most enjoyable and relaxed summer I have ever had with my kids.

Parenting has definite perks. All the things we said we would do when we got older are at our fingertips, but how often do we play, chill, or stay up late? Valerie Bertinelli gave a great response to a distraught woman with picky eaters not cleaning their plates and whining for dessert. She replied, "Why does it have to be a rule to finish everything on your plate? Do you? ... Kids won't starve if they don't finish their meals and they don't need dessert every night. But every once in a while, freak them out and give them that scoop of ice cream before dinner!" Excellent advice for myself, I thought—"Girlfriend, you have got to lighten up."

This is not throwing order to the wind. Establishing rules and routines are, as researchers note, essential to a child's feeling of security. Knowing what is coming makes children feel more in control and less likely to be irritable, impatient, and all the rest of those i-words. It's loosening the rigidness that makes the difference.

A few days ago, at summer high noon, the kids collectively said they were not hungry, until someone saw the ice cream. Suddenly, they had appetites. On a whim, I said, "Do you want dessert first?" They were about to faint. "All right," I said, "I officially declare this Dessert First Day." And with that, we enjoyed: we savored, we sloshed, and we slurped that ice cream as it should be.

This was fun.

GOT JOY?
A MOTHER OF NINE FOUND SOME

Recently, I've been thinking about joy. So often as mothers we focus on the functional, out of necessity, and forget the fun. Somehow we're missing the joy and need to get it back.

So I emailed my friend, Ingrid Sorensen, a mother of nine who loves being a mom (most days), and who has found a way to find joy (on the tail end of many children). Here's what she said:

"Over the years I noticed something: my dear husband is super good at finding things he loves to do, then making time to do them. In the midst of stressful work and life, he has FUN. Though I needed that too, I sat around waiting—for many years and several children—for it to somehow magically happen. Newsflash! My kids nor my husband—bless their well-meaning hearts—were never going to say 'Wow, you need some fun in your life. Here, let me do (blank) for you.' It was up to ME.

So, I bit the bullet. I researched where I could take a ballet class, a dream from my youth, found one and filled out the forms right there. POW! That fast I became, and still am, a ballet student. So what if I'm a 40-year old in a college-level ballet class with a bunch of 18 and 20 year olds? Who cares?! I'm happy, fulfilled, and have something joyful to look forward to twice a week while NOT thinking about the 8 zillion other things I have to do. The huge dorky smile on my face from ballet lasts all day. Suddenly, the effort of finding early morning child care, jumping through hoops to qualify for the class, and coming home to being a little behind on morning chores is so worth it."

Three cheers for Ingrid! And for all mothers who are reading this and beginning to think, Maybe I can take that class. Maybe I can sign up for that half-marathon. Today, brainstorm fun activities, events, classes, or projects you would love to do. Then schedule a few hours a week to make them happen.

Joy is not about self-focus, absolutely. But it *is* about living presently and purposefully, showing your children that being a mom is fun. Add that spoonful of joy to your motherhood schedule and watch how frothy and delicious your daily life becomes.

LIGHTENING UP IN MOTHERHOOD

At the start of a new year, I had some anxiety about how I was doing as a mother. While making goals for our children and myself, it was easy to see many needed changes (which possibly related to my need for chocolate-covered pretzels. By the handful.)

But thankfully, before I could open the bag, I began reading Chieko Okazaki's, *Lighten Up*.

What a fabulous book! If you want to feel great about yourself and your abilities, read it. I was drawn to the chapter, "Motherhood: Less Guilt, More Joy," that shares the following:

"I have received a startling education on the amount of inappropriate guilt literally hundreds of wonderful women feel about motherhood ... women with infertility problems feel guilty that they cannot bear children. Mothers worry that they have too many children, or too few. Many others worry because they are not perfect mothers or don't have perfect children ... and [relating to children's poor choices] even more personal guilt that springs from the feeling that they have somehow failed...

"I strongly feel that we should expect struggles and imperfections in this life. The most realistic expectation we can make of ourselves is to do our best. We should not expect to control outcomes, either for ourselves or our children."

What a relief! Suddenly I felt light and clear about being a mother, and not so bad about making my four-year-old go back to her bed (after the fortieth time of being up). I began thinking about all the good things I do with and for my children. How last week we bought red "mini mailboxes" for each child, complete with mini flag, so we can give them love messages. How I had played ponies, did horse puzzles, danced to their favorite song, colored and glued, made a tasty lunch, and cuddled them before naps.

I encourage you to make an "I Am a Fabulous Mother" list and put it in a lovely and easily accessible place. Write each reason that you are a fabulous mother in an "I" statement. This is because too often we do not recognize and own our efforts in a personal way. Stand tall and say what you do well as a mother!

For fun (and possibly debate), here is the beginning of my fabulous mother list (that I will surely read to my children during Family Night—all 429 of them):

1. I apologize. When I've blown it, I say sorry and move on.

2. I do floor time with the children every day. Though I must admit that puzzles and play dough after fifteen years is not doing it for me, I focus on the joy it's bringing to them (and a great book reward for me later on).

3. I can be beaten in Scrabble. This gives them a great sense of accomplishment and makes them feel that they are, frankly, invincible.

4. I delegate. These sweet children help in everything. From putting in a load of laundry to loading

the dishwasher, each child down to our four-year-old help with the home.

5. I am affectionate. Whether it's first thing in the morning or last thing at night, whether it's touch or talk, they are loved, loved, loved. Doesn't matter that my oldest is fourteen, smooches abound in this house.

6. I refuse to hear negative talk about my cooking. I feel that this is a service rendered for their future wives. As soon as a negative word starts to form, they know it's a double portion of dinner for them.

7. I love their father. Around the children I keep appropriately tight-lipped when my sweet honey DRIVES ME ABSOLUTELY BONKERS. But about the great stuff (and making fun of the bonkers stuff), I let it fly.

8. I have chilled out in the "über structure" department. This past month my husband and I "eased up" on during-the-week children's play dates (usually reserved for Fridays and Saturdays). They are now allowed one on Wednesday IF their rooms are tidy, their homework to that point is done, their laundry is completed, and anything else I can think of that needs to get done while they are motivated.

9. I take time for me. Whether it's exercise, reading, enjoying my special treats without mini-mouths breathing on them, I teach them that a relaxed mom is a happy mom, and a ready-to-say-yes-to-their-requests mom.

10. I read good books that make me remember to enjoy the process and season of raising my young children without ripping their little lips off.

Remember that *our own* personal manifestation of motherhood—the good, the bad and the downright annoying—is a gift and a blessing that we uniquely give to our children.

MOTHER

PATIENT WITH THE REAL

THREE UNPLEASANT REALITIES
OF MOTHERHOOD WE CAN ACCEPT

In the journey to become a stellar mother, there are simple but unpleasant truths that happy, veteran mothers have learned to accept. I share but three.

The Flaky Mom. At some point you will be the Flaky Mom, and more than likely to mainly one person. It's a strange but true phenomena. This person will not see you as your typical fabulous self because for some reason when you are with said person, suddenly you can't remember to meet them for lunch, or to share dinner duty for the PTA, or to pick up their six children from a school play practice on time.

But that's OK. Because being the Flaky Mom allows you to pay it forward when on the receiving end of another flakester. Like myself. For over two years one of my friends endured, saint-like, my hormonal forgetfulness. I apologized profusely. I confessed I didn't know why it was only to her. I even brought treats and trinkets as a symbolic olive branch, but things did not change with my brain. I often wondered how she was so patient. And then I paid it forward and found out.

I became friends with a fabulously wonderful woman who was experiencing the Flaky Mom syndrome. Initially, when she would forget, miss, or complicate appointments, I became frustrated. But then a voice of reason said Alamo-like, "Remember Ann." That one thought immediately changed my attitude.

Now I take the flakesters in stride because I know how often I've been the offender, and how soon I will likely be one again.

Being Less Than. Whether it's your kids, your waistline, the size of your house, the make of your car, or worry over how many awards your child will win at school, at some point, as a mother, you will feel less than. A few years ago I spoke to a large business conference on tidying up your life, at home and at work. It went spectacularly. So much so that women followed me out to the car to help stow my speaking materials. As I opened the front passenger door, I was greeted with a ketchup drip, nay, a river, going from the door handle down to the bottom of the door. From my driver's side vantage point it was at such an angle that I hadn't seen the little gift my son had left me the night before.

I still remember the silence that fell and how one woman (obviously a veteran mother) laughed and made a joke about children and messes, then left me to my embarrassment. This inevitability of being "less than" is one to learn quickly because it will happen often. And when it does, simply remember that as mothers, that's part of the package. Own it and soon you'll be laughing along with the other mothers at the ketchup river. As one woman said, her friends told her she had no ego. She said no, I have teenagers.

You will drop the ball. You can't be all things to all people, most especially within your own family. That's intended. We have to make choices, and because of that we will make mistakes. Some of them will be small. Like the tooth fairy forgetting to show up. This has happened so often at our house that now our children look forward to the Tooth Fairy getting lost in a storm, being unable to find the tooth (though it's under a pillow), or accidentally giving money to a sibling who didn't lose a tooth. They know if she makes a mistake, they make bank. One tooth cost the fairy a solid fiver with a Cold Stone coupon. She was pretty punctual after that.

Other mistakes will be bigger. Forgetting a child at the ball park. Setting a punishment that was too harsh. Or ignoring signs in a child that warned something was seriously wrong. Sometimes dropping the parental ball will be a very, very painful experience, but also a learning lesson if we choose. We can show our children how to pick up the dropped ball, yet again, and continue to move forward.

As I said, there are many motherhood realities that we can accept and even embrace. Hopefully, you can allow yourself to nod and give yourself permission to do the same, before you find a ketchup river on your car door.

WE ARE A HAPPY FAMILY...RIGHT?

Twice a year my church has a large televised conference teaching basic joyful life principles, especially about families. One conference was particularly terrific—until we actually involved our family. As we listened to the wise words of speakers, in the background bickering, snickering, and outright contention were pretty much the modus operandi.

The apex came when one of the speakers said that the most important thing in life is our family. Just then our nine-year-old stood at the doorway of the room and announced, "I hate this family!" then slammed her bedroom door. We found out this outburst was completely justified because it had been about the design of a blanket fort and she had not been able to have it her way.

Sigh.

I thought about what the speaker had said. Did that mean we were doing it wrong because my children were being pills? Dealing with the matter at hand, we paused from watching the conference and talked with the girls (after a calming time out) about how the key to getting good things was behaving in a good way, etc., etc., etc. Ironically, not an hour later we enjoyed relative peace as the girls played in their blanket fort, the dog sighed contentedly, and I made a yummy big brunch with the hum of family chit chat surrounding me.

All was right with the world.

And it hit me—that's a family. One minute you want to pull out your hair (or theirs), and the next you're roasting marshmallows and thinking how to make the moment last. So if there is some contention, a little door slamming, and some good old-fashioned sticking out of tongues, know that you're doing just fine.

Meanwhile, take a deep breath, give a hug, share a smile, and say something good about each family member as often as you can. They may not respond in kind but you will have set the tone. Families have stretching and growing pains, some stages lasting longer than others. So put on a smile, see the good in your stage, and move on with joy.

SOMETIMES LIFE IS LIKE THAT

The other morning began like this ... the children were late getting up (despite my coaxing) because of the "summer is in the air, don't want to go to bed" syndrome (or so I thought).

I had been up life coaching online until midnight when my baby, who was starting a cold, woke up and would not go back to sleep. Exhausted, at 3:00 A.M., I passed the baton to my husband, while my other daughter decided to play musical beds until 5:00 A.M.

Exhausted, I corralled the children downstairs for breakfast. Pulling down the Cheerios I realized someone had left the bag open and down came the rain of cereal over literally half the kitchen floor. As soon as I cleaned it up, while getting cereal for the other children, my four-year-old bumped her cereal bowl, creating one of those splattery, upturned, it goes everywhere messes, on the other side of the kitchen floor (and kitchen table, and kitchen chairs).

Cleaning this up—with gentle, encouraging phrases like "YOU'RE GONNA MISS THE BUS, HUSTLE YOUR BUSTLE NOWWWWW"—I realized that the chores from last night had not been completed. My daughter couldn't find the "right" shirt to wear and was in a tear-filled breakdown, and my other son who had sworn to finish his homework had instead joined everyone else and AT THE HAND OF THEIR FATHER listened intently to a sports game on the radio

143

downstairs (the penny drops on the non-chore doing).

By this time, the Nazi in me had taken over and I began barking commands: "HAIR, GEL .... YOU. BACKPACK, SNACK... NO TREATS. YOU—SHOES ARE NOT AN OPTION AT SCHOOL."

And then I heard that sound that makes us all freeze in mid-air—the sound of a rumbling school bus passing our driveway. In one of those classic mother moments that you swear you will never experience, I said in an I-told-you-so yelling tone, "YOU'VE MISSED YOUR BUS. GET YOUR FANNIES TO THE STOP SIGN AND STAY TOGETHER."

Ahh, family togetherness.

The point of this is that it's been a week of mothering. And though most of the time it's worked out, unbelievably and in a way I can't fathom, sometimes, like yesterday, it goes to the dogs (or the kitchen floor).

So my thought here is two-fold: life's moments aren't always going to be balanced and beautiful, even when you're practicing balanced and beautiful principles (or even teaching them, creating products about them and talking about them on TV or radio). Because, as you know, there would be no growth, and that would be boring—never mind give me nothing to write about.

So, in tribute to mothers everywhere, thank you for your unspoken patience in *days like that*, and support of what all mothers do—especially for me as a cereal-cleaning, command-barking mother.

PLAYING MOTHERHOOD, ONE PASSAGE AT A TIME

Saturday was rough. My kids spent the better part of the day in a no-win conversation going something like, "He is being RUDE, he took my blaaaaahhh" (the rest was lost in unintelligible wails). To which the other responded, "Well, he was SO MEAN" (dramatic facial expression). "He said blah, blah, blaaaahhh, and THAT'S RUDE." As the day wore on, so did my nerves. And by nightfall I was teetering on the edge of Mom's Officially Losing Her Temper.

I hadn't heard more than two syllables of the bathtub "blaaahhh" when I marched in and said, "That's it—you're out—no Racer points—you're in bed—don't think about treats—not even a glass of water—no talking, no reading, no blaahing—this is RIDICULOUS" (dramatic facial expressions and hand gestures). Officially, Mom had blown it.

Janene Wolsey Baadsgaard, in her book *Families Who Laugh ... Last* relates this letter exchange between parent and teacher.

"Dear Parent: Please do not send Jason to school partially clothed.

To which the parent responded, "Dear Teacher: I send Jason to school fully clothed. What does he look like when he gets there?"

We do our best. We feed our children nutritious foods, help them get enough rest, finish homework and learn responsibility—all on time and within budget. Some of us help them regularly floss, but let's not go there. And then things out of our control—and even some things in our control—fall through, come apart, or explode.

In motherhood, we will blow it. Sometimes discreetly, sometimes in front of the entire PTA. How many women have come out of a Mother's Day church service feeling that they are a failure, that the bar is too high so why try? We cannot be perfect in mothering, period. But we can take each experience and squeeze the learning out of it. We can look at life as a process and allow ourselves to live it. And we can allow our children to grow without superficial expectations when there are plenty of real ones. By doing so, we teach our children that trying our best and saying we're sorry are two of the most important principles we can live by.

What is more important is not that we blew it, but how we handle blowing it. Baadsgaard likens this to "selective sight reading" when playing a difficult piano piece. In a recital, when the parts get too hard, you have to choose the notes you can play and move on.

We are playing "life" for the first time and as it gets more complicated we can't possibly play all the notes. But as we are presented with particular passages over and over, we get better and better, mastering areas one passage at a time.

In our children's emotional development, being an example of growth is more positively life-changing than pretending false perfection.

A few minutes after my eruption that night, my son called to me from the hallway. Initially, I felt to say, "Back in bed, mister." But instead I asked, "What did you need?"

He said, "Come sit on my bed, please." Very parent-like, he said, "I was thinking about how you were angry and how I made you angry and it made me sad. I'm sorry I made you feel that way."

In that moment, I knew that at another time he had seen me practice and fail—had seen me learn, grow and move on. And now, he was practicing too.

ARE YOU A 10,000 HOUR MOTHER?

Recently, Malcolm Gladwell who is a columnist for the *New Yorker* shared the concept of "deliberate practice." In his research of highly successful people, he discovered that most of them—no matter their profession, hobby, or pursuit—had several compelling things in common.

One of the first of these was that each had "practiced" about 10,000 hours, which equals about ten years. He likened that number to society "greats" such as Michael Jordan or the Beatles. What made them successful is that they got an early start in life on their 10,000 hours of playing music or basketball, and spent hours doing it every day. These hours weren't simply showing up. This was a deliberate practice of focusing efforts and fine-tuning weaknesses. As skills improved, these successful people would continually look to what needed more improvement, and then immediately got busy.

This concept struck a chord with me. Mostly because after almost twenty years of mothering, I wondered if my motherhood had been one of deliberate practice. Like many mothers, I reflected whether my daily activities added up to something measurably meaningful. And meaningful to me personally. Had I been merely passing time or was I truly engaged, rejoicing in my triumphs, and consciously improving the not-so-triumphant?

Mr. Gladwell added that for those mega-successes, talent ultimately didn't matter. It helped to be sure, but talent was not more important than overcoming difficulty and being consistent. Those who wanted it more, who sacrificed more, and felt more passionate about their chosen field, became more successful. The difficulty and consistency included an opportunity to work harder, meaning longer days or hours (such as summer practice or extended work or school days), and creating a hunger. The hunger derived from negative or difficult experiences—perhaps someone had said the person couldn't succeed, or the person considered the same possibility. Either way, it created a feeling of hunger, of "I'm going to make this happen."

As I thought on these things, I happened to look at the wall where we had recently hung our children's individual portraits. As I gazed at their faces, I couldn't help but feel emotional remembering all I'd been through with each of these children so far—the sleepless nights, behavior challenges, and life discipline. From instilling personal values of spiritual foundations, integrity, and obedience, to learning matter-of-fact life skills such as cleaning a bathroom or putting on deodorant every day, I thought of all the loving, living, and learning we had shared together. Did that count as my 10,000 hours? Was I, in fact, a successful mother?

Actual experiences flashed through my mind. Like when our two boys went sledding, and how our twelve-year-old got his four-wheeler stuck in the snow and our fifteen-year-old calmly and knowingly undid the winch, hooking up and pulling him out. Or when my nine-year-old daughter read a story to her two younger sisters then helped them brush their teeth and tucked them in bed like a pro. Or when my youngest finally started sleeping in her own bed. Or one son happily shared the progress on his growing manly armpit hair. And another son said in his prayers every single day, "We thank thee for such wonderful parents". And finally, how after school each of our children hurried through the door and the first person they looked for was me.

Am I a successful mother? Absolutely. And, like most every mother, I've had more than 10,000 hours of sacrifice and opportunities to work harder, and great passion and hunger borne of difficult experiences. I believe each of us can, with thousands of other mothers, stand next to any of the "greats" of society. By virtue of our choice and dedication, we can acknowledge that individually and collectively, we as mothers are a success.

DEALING WITH MOTHERHOOD GUILT

Whether it comes from our children, our spouse, or the PTA chair, it's guaranteed as a mother we're going to feel guilty about something. Learn how to avoid three guilt traps with effective self-questions.

The Guilt Sponge. We're human so we will make mistakes. Healthy guilt helps us realize when we need to apologize and change. Unhealthy guilt, however, makes us feel inept, brings low self-esteem, and a desire to consume copious amounts of carbs. A simple way to determine the type of guilt is to ask, "Is it mine?"

If it is your fault/beef/issue, pick up the guilt sponge and deal with it. If it isn't, don't pick it up! One of our friends had a son getting married this summer. Apparently, the happy duo didn't realize that the page of invitation addresses from his mother had more addresses on the back of the sheet. Oops. Instead of immersing herself in guilt over those who were dissed, the mother simply sent out a short email that said, this is what happened, sorry, know that you're invited and we'd love to see you. No cry fest, no anger bout, no guilt-induced food binge.

The "Less Than" Syndrome. Looking around you see accomplished women, clean homes, and tidy yards. Women who run for office, after training for a half-marathon, right after they bake a batch of cookies. Get over it. If you feel less than, ask yourself, "Is this important to me?" You probably don't want to do or be half the things you see women do or be. But because they do them well, you feel less than.

Instead, try being a "B+" in life. It's fabulous! Enjoy not being a neurotic "A" in things that aren't vital, and you'll have more quality of life. Years ago my preschool daughter was asked to bring a poster to celebrate being "Blossom of the Week." Good intentions aside, the poster was forgotten until ten minutes before carpool. Bustling into action, she and I made one barely in time, except that my carpool friend was not that impressed. I'm sad to admit that I fretted, I worried, and I felt "less than" for an entire fifteen minutes until the phone rang. It was the preschool teacher telling me it was indeed the cutest poster that she had ever seen. From that pathetic experience I learned to relax and remember that it's a poster (or a science project, or cupcakes), not a Nobel Peace Prize.

The Mary Poppins Mother. Mary was practically perfect in every way with the perfect thing handy in her bottomless bag at any moment.

Can you say, FAIRYTALE?

So the neighbor lady has children in music, dance, sports, and honor roll. That doesn't mean you need to. Stop trying to be the neighbor lady and ask yourself, "What mothering do my children need?" My daughter was once enrolled in a dance class that I could quickly see was a wrong fit—they were trophy-oriented and she needed expression and enjoyment. So at the last minute I switched her to another studio and she loved it. In fact, after a tough day at school, I could visibly see dance relieving her tension—laughing and dancing it away. That's what hobbies should do.

So next time inappropriate guilt threatens, try one of these suggestions and before you know it, you'll be guilt-free.

SAYING WHEN

In the movie "Regarding Henry," a high-powered lawyer suffers a gunshot to the brain and afterward has to learn basic motor and life skills all over again. When he returns to work, the secretary pours him some tea and tells him to say when. As the milk is rising rapidly in the cup, she realizes the need to explain the concept and tells him, "When you've had enough, you say when."

Recently, I needed to be reminded when to say when. It was one of those crazy busy weeks, filled with running kids to afterschool activities (the times and days of which kept changing), homework projects, deep cleaning, and attempting to tackle the yard. Never mind Scouts, dinner on the table, and of course, trying to exercise. (Why can't running kids around count as aerobic exercise?)

Exhausted from being pulled in too many different directions, I breathed my way through it until Thursday. And then, I rebelled. A switch went off inside me and I literally could not try to make every minute productive for one more second. After emailing a great friend that very thought—and asking her humorously if I should take the weekend off, she emailed back and wisely agreed (Take a few weekends off, she insisted).

So this time, I did.

That very day instead of being uber-functional mom, I took a nap with my baby, watched an episode of Agatha

Christie's Hercule Poirot, and enjoyed a Skinny Cow chocolate truffle bar.

Best. Day. Ever.

In fact, this act of letting down allowed new ideas and projects to surface. So many that in my creative excitement I had to email them to that same friend (who promptly sent me video clips of Back to the Future's "Hello, McFly?" to remind me of my earlier bitter diatribe and self-promise TO RELAX).

It is an eternal truth, one that I cannot quite get through my stubborn head: alternating busy with letting down creates a yin-yang balance of the soul. Every single time I regularly allow myself to slow down, enjoy, and just be, I automatically become more rejuvenated, creative, and joyful.

I invite you to find a time to let down and let go. Do something fun, even when laundry calls to you (simply shut the door). And I'm not suggesting every minute of every day (I wish). But find a time and an activity that lets you relax and gets that smile back on your face.

For me, I'm back to practicing what I preach on a daily basis. And as for the "few weekends" my friend suggested, I already have an overnighter booked at our favorite hotel.

Here's to more rejuvenation.

MOTHER

HELP CHILDREN GROW

STOP BEING A BOSSY PANTS

The other day I asked my daughter Chloe to be my Sous Chef; meaning, she would help me with dinner. She is the "cooker" of our family who loves to bake and do all things with the oven. So there we were, making lasagna and these darling lemon mini Bundt cakes with this fabulous new dealy wheely pan. She is wearing her apron. She is ecstatic. She is officially cooking!

And what do I do? Be a cook hog! From assembling the noodles to scraping out the batter bowl I forgot to simply demonstrate and instead pretty much took over the whole deal IN THE INTEREST OF TIME. I was reminded, yet again, to back off and let the little lady do the work. She's in third grade and can learn for herself. And if I ever want to realize my dream of sitting on the couch while my children slave over the stove, it begins now.

Do you find yourself doing this? We want our children to become self-sufficient and Future Stellar Adults. But then we have to get the girls to dance, or pick up someone from school, and it's chop-chop, and I'll just do it myself.

For once, try doing it differently. Allow the bathroom to look semi-clean even though your child has been at it for two hours. Celebrate that the school project supposedly resembling the Pyramid of Giza looks more like a melted marshmallow snowman. Ignore the plethora of wrong notes on the should-be-recital-ready piano piece. It's all part of the learning process.

Each year our children decorate the Christmas tree and each year I find myself less inclined to fill in the gaps. What does it matter? They're learning better how to decorate the tree and their self-esteem is soaring. Of course, it's entirely coincidental that very large gift boxes are strategically placed in various spots in front of the tree.

Later the same daughter and I attempted to make Cream of Wheat. At the last minute I needed to flat iron someone's hair for school. When I came back to the kitchen she had not used the one cup of grain that I had told her, but instead, three cups. Her response to the thick, unwieldy mess was to be expected—crying, she ran from the kitchen into her room and slammed the door. Calmly, I explained to her that (a) we could buy more Cream of Wheat, and (b) it was all part of the learning-to-cook process (I bit my tongue about anything else).

So this week I encourage you to make yourself stand back and not be a bossy pants. Simply oversee and demonstrate, and help only when your children truly need it. There will be mistakes. There will be tears. But there will be growth.

LOSE THE HOVER MOTHER

I tell the following hovering experience for a reason. Mainly, because I'm desperate to believe that there are other mothers who hover, helicopter, or like me, land the aircraft and are ready to invade.

My sweet daughter (first daughter, maybe that's it) had cheer camp one year. She and her best friend from the previous year—who were now at different schools— had done a cheer camp each year. It was their special time to bond and connect.

They got together that initial Monday, not having seen each other in a long time, and this sweet gal would hardly give my daughter the time of day. She stood away from her, barely smiled, and hardly talked at all. My daughter tried to take her hand, like they usually did, but the friend put her hand in her pocket and moved away.

My heart was breaking for my sweet Chelsea. I thought, *This is one of those piercing moments of childhood, when you grow apart from dear friends and no longer share the same interests...blah, blah, blah.* I almost called my husband about it—this really put me out all morning— "the loss" as I was about to name it.

Thankfully, I didn't call him. Thankfully, I have at least grown up a wee bit in my middle age to not have to be so mired in my daughter's young and uncomplicated life (that I feel so driven to complicate).

And did I mention she is only seven years old?

Two days later, heading out to cheer camp once again, this friend's mother told me that they didn't realize until Monday evening that her daughter had a FEVER and was SICK AS A DOG that day. At that moment, as if on cue, her daughter bounded up to my car, her usual smiley, happy self. Immediately, she and my daughter made plans for an extended play date the next day.

The moral to the story here is: butt out. Allowing our children to go through the perceived pangs of childhood without the overdone feelings of motherhood is a healthy thing. Sure the validation is needed, sure my daughter felt something was up. My hugs to her and a little fun time with Mom on that tough first day surely helped. But THANK GOODNESS I didn't call up her mother immediately and find out why her daughter wasn't kind to my daughter. Thank goodness I let things be, for one tiny moment, and let it play itself out.

This week, enjoy your children's lives as a mother and not a helicopter.

THE POWER OF THE KEY WORD

Each of my four children was born with abnormal hearing. Through exhaustive research I have discovered that they are afflicted with what I call SDRS, or Selective Dog-Like Response Systems. Similar to Pavlovian responses, though more sophisticated, my children hear entire conversations but only respond to particular words.

For example, I will clearly say, "Boys, please pick up the Legos and put them in your Lego tub."

What they hear translates to "Blah blah Legos, blah blah Legos." To which they respond, "Hey, my LEGOS!"

Interestingly, I've noticed a similar disorder in their father. I say, "Honey will you take out the garbage and put softener salts in the tank?"

And what he hears is "Blah blah, take out blah blah tank." What I get is chow mien and a reading on our water heater.

Several years ago, I asked myself, *Where am I going wrong?* The future looked bleak indeed, when, like a toddler's rejected pancake, it hit me: I was trying to be logical. I was trying to make sense. You see, I had forgotten I was dealing with men and small children (OK, partially kidding there). So I devised a new strategy—only using words that motivated, that contained two syllables or less, and that required no logic whatsoever.

For example, I now say, "Boys, please clean your room with ice cream and you can empty the dishwasher treats." This gets their attention.

Which leads to, "What, Mom?" or, "What was that?" This is big, really big, because I get what every mother wants —eyeballs. Now they are committed—they have acknowledged I exist, and I have verified their ear drums are indeed functioning.

The ultimate benefit of this technique is that, though the key words change, the principle remains the same. Sure, they graduate to bigger words like "keys to the car," and "remote control," but no matter the age, the response is generally the same—a response. And in my book, that is big.

Recently, I retrieved my four-year-old son from the neighborhood preschool. After joining the moms outside, I was juggling my one-year-old daughter and two-year-old son when the latter wriggled free, running diaper naked down the street. Quickly, I had to choose— chase him in thick clogs, balancing a flailing infant or use a key word? Technique and vanity won, and grappling for the right word I screamed, "Ethan, come here." He ran. "Ethan, come HERE." He laughed. *Think, think*—the nice neighbor ladies watched with ping-pong head motions. My final serve, "Ethan, ICE CREAM." He stopped in his tracks, turned about, and ran his diapered fanny right into my arms.

THE JOY IN LETTING CHILDREN WORK IT OUT

Recently our family solved a mystery. In preparation for Thanksgiving, I had purchased some sparkling cider and while bringing in groceries, one of the bottles had fallen and crashed, leaving us two, and no plans for a return trip to the store. The morning before turkey day I woke up to see one of the precious remaining bottles sitting by the fridge, opened, partially empty. This, with nary an explanation as to why we would now be deprived of our traditional cider for the big celebration (gross insult and weighty error that it was).

As I asked the children nearby if they had opened the bottle, all claimed innocence and ignorance. For some reason, hearing the repeated phrase, "I dunno know, wasn't me," put me over the edge. Suddenly, it was if a fast rewinding history of similar moments went through my brain, moments when something that I needed/used/liked/thought was vitally important was suddenly destroyed/opened/used/gone. And then it happened.

I decided to follow through.

Rather than push for an answer—then lecture not to touch what isn't yours, blah, blah, blah—I said that the bottle didn't matter so much as the principle. I calmly stated that this kind of behavior of taking or using or eating whatever was spontaneously desired needed to stop. In order to do that, I needed to know who it was that had opened the bottle. Still no one confessed. I then announced that everyone would sit at the table today until the person who had done so would admit it. Then I peacefully went about tidying the house.

While cleaning, I did what any good parent would do and carefully eavesdropped on their discussion, which was highly instructive. They went around the table, each sharing why they could or could not have done it. Like something out of an Agatha Christie novel, they began eliminating, BY THEMSELVES, who could have done it. A few times I was summoned to note that they had agreed to eliminate certain people from suspicion. The discussion moved from the table to another room as they began to fold laundry (I figured they may as well multi-task while sleuthing).

Ultimately, it came down to two people, well-known for similar behaviors in the past. Now at this point, I was caught up in the criminal investigation myself and seriously could not determine who it was. My suspicion was with the elder brother, but it was curious that the bottle was not completely emptied and hidden, which did not fit with his profile. The younger son didn't have an outstanding history of such acts, but then, we did nickname him "Stealth" because he is always the first to silently disappear when any form of work is required.

Time was ticking and the field was narrowing. You could feel the peer pressure in the room as the children continued to analyze each story and response. The tension reached its ironic and tragic apex: the eldest son in question had a project to complete and had mixed plaster for it right before the "inquiry" began. He ran to the plaster, saw it had irreversibly hardened, and became momentarily inconsolable (no more plaster, no completed project). Right then the younger brother in question reached said project, saw the hardened plaster, heard the elder son's plight, and actually began to tear up.

After I expressed my condolences on the plaster, I left to put in another load of laundry. Suddenly, there it was, a sound of sweetness. I peeked in the room to see my eldest son hugging my younger son and telling him that it was alright and that it feels better to tell the truth. The middle son was quietly adding epithets such as, "We're proud of you for telling the truth...just don't go getting a big head or anything."

As I realized my youngest had spilled the beans and was the Cider Cypher, I recognized two amazing outcomes from this experience. One, how vital it is that we allow our children to work things out in their own way more often. And two, how surprisingly compassionate and sweet my boys could be. At the appropriate moment, my husband and I entered the room and shared how proud we were of them all, and life went back to the regular rhythm.

My husband and I turned to leave and smiled at each other. Another magical parenting moment that, appropriately, did not require us as parents.

RESPONDING CREATIVELY

This week I was reminded of an experience that had happened years ago. My eleven-year-old son had decided to run away. He was extremely angry, had semi-run away before (enough to frighten me), and had had enough of the chores, restrictions, family time, yada yada yada—and that was it—he was outta here.

And in fact, he informed me that he would be JUST FINE because he had learned how to camp at Scout camp (suddenly I despised Scouts).

So there my son was, putting on his backpack with all the accessories. And the more he talked, the more excited he got, explaining in detail how to use the stove, and all the cool gadgets he and his father had bought.

Knowing the disabilities my son has dealt with, I was concerned. But the more I could see he really WAS prepared and really COULD camp for days, the more I started to panic.

Taking a deep breath, I did the only rational thing a woman could do. I called my husband. He said, "Whoa, I'll be home in a jiff. Let me think creatively too. "

Then I had a thought. As he prepped his gear, I casually threw out, "I'm really going to miss you. We're having pizza tonight and your favorite ice cream. But that's OK, we'll see you soon."

Then I made sure he heard me order his favorite pepperoni pizza from his favorite place, *with* root beer. To this point he had already spent a good half hour of stomping around. Combined with the pizza thing I noticed his step slowing, that he kept having to come back for "more gear," but the zeal was definitely dissipating. Now he wasn't so sure how to get out of the deal.

Then my husband walked in. He lamented our son was leaving too, and casually mentioned to watch for the cougars that roam our wooded area. And then he spoke objectively but powerfully about bears, wild hogs and even kidnappers, who before you could say boo, would take him across the state line and he would never be seen again.

About five minutes later, with pizza coming up the drive, our son announced that he had changed his mind and wouldn't be going after all. No one said a word about his previous plans, and I simply added, "Great, we're so glad you're staying. Grab some paper plates for the pizza."

I thought of this experience because several times lately this same son has been an incredible help and amazingly kind. He has been a wonderful caregiving helper to my little ones and sensitive to those around him. But raising him has required that we often respond creatively in order not to lose him in an authoritarian fight of us versus him. And thankfully, he is turning into a wonderful young man.

Sometimes, between hormones and everyday stresses, we can tend toward an all-or-nothing solution with our children. When what would work better for both parties is a soft, creative response. Like once when my children were yelling at each other (you're gonna think things are GREAT at my house), I said to them, "Stop yelling at your brother—that's my job." They started laughing, and it diffused the situation.

If you creatively respond even once, that's one more time than you would have. And after that it gets easier—certainly not that you will do it all the time, but more often than before. The stress is released, the atmosphere becomes calm, and future stress is eliminated because it isn't mounting into a later explosion. Today, try a creative response!

IF YOU GIVE A KID A COOKIE, HE'LL WANT A LEGO

While I was reading *Parenting with Love and Logic*, my seven-year-old pored over his Lego magazine. "Hey," he shouted, "this Lego is only eighty dollars."

Really? "Only *eighty* dollars," I repeated. And indicated that would be possibly out of the question. Understanding but undeterred, minutes later he shouted, "Hey! This one is only forty dollars and that's cheaper." Understanding but undeterred, I followed Love and Logic advice: validate his vision.

"Wow," I said, "that *is* a neat battering ram." I smiled. I didn't squelch his dream with something like, "Are you kidding mister? When I was your age I got a hand-me-down Barbie with one go-go-boot and no arms, so don't come crying to me with your Lego troubles."

That said, I went in for the Love and Logic kill. "Son," I smiled, "how do you want to earn that Lego?" He stared as if I was speaking Swahili. Translating, I enlightened him on a few economic factors; a day job, three months of piano lessons, etc. In reply, he pulled out a cookie recipe, two eggs, and expensive vanilla. With the self-made cookies and a neighbor partner, he went door-to-door while I walked inconspicuously behind. After forty-five minutes they were sold out with six dollars in change. He and his friend subtracted one dollar for ingredients and, through serious negotiations, split the remainder.

Past generations feared illnesses such as chicken pox and influenza because it caused physical death. In our current gimme-now generation, many children (never parents, of course) suffer from a deadlier illness. Namely, entitlement—which brings motivational death. Without taking ownership for what they want or who they're to become, our children will think life is one big Lego gift, one after another.

Authors Cline and Fay state, "To help children gain responsibility, we must offer that child opportunities to be responsible." Unwittingly, we as loving parents who experienced sacrifice and want to protect our children from the same, now sacrifice, not the money but their opportunity for growth gained from desperately wanting and determinedly doing.

This is not child labor or throwing kids in a pool and yelling swim. To wit, we equally matched my son's earnings and accompanied him on the next cookie outing—five of us on the four-wheeler, inconspicuously. No matter the form, a parent's contribution says, "I believe you will succeed."

Giving back the responsibility takes follow-through and selectivity; not every item is buy-it-yourself. You'll know a special item when it's all they talk about, think about, and whine about. They don't whine about bagels. Involve them by asking responsibility-giving questions: what can you make/do/sell to earn the money? Talk it through, enthusiastically, and why not? This is your possible future retirement at stake.

In a confusing move, my son used his cookie money to buy our family pizza. He said it made him happy. And that he wanted mom and dad to have more money to buy him a bike.

MOTHER

MAKE SURE THEY KNOW

"MINI LOVES" FOR KIDS: POWERFUL AND SIMPLE

Recently I set some parenting goals and was surprised with what I learned. One of my goals was to connect with each child daily, and ideally for at least ten minutes per child. That may not sound like much but with several children and busy schedules, it added up. And it helped me see how often a few children received much more than ten minutes, while others were hit and miss, depending on the day.

First, I learned not to feel guilty about not having more time but to enjoy the time I did spend with each child. And I consciously did! What became ideal for me was to love in the moment—"mini loves", such as a text, a smile, a conversation, a hug, etc. And doing them right then: after school, as we made dinner together, sitting on my bed while other children gathered for family prayer, etc. It didn't have to be a big block of time, but with consistent "mini love" connections throughout the day.

Second, I also thoroughly enjoyed one-on-one time. This wasn't daily, but divided up into several smaller time chunks during the week. What terrific memory makers! My thirteen-year-old son had entered a First Chapter novel contest for a teen author boot camp. Can I tell you how fabulous it was to share that experience together? He wrote the text, then I helped him revise it, and we mutually enjoyed the collaboration. This

173

interspersed one-on-one time also motivated me, though tired, to make peppermint scones with my I-love-to-bake daughter who is nine. We had a great time, chatting and mixing a simple kids' recipe, and the family loved the results.

Lastly, I looked at their love-share like our pediatrician told me to view my children's nutrition—by the week! If one child received thirty minutes of attention one day, it worked fine to focus on another child more fully the next, but still give the first one mini loves. The kids seemed more satiated due to the larger time chunks of togetherness, and were more easily satisfied with the mini loves in the meantime.

Congratulate yourself on all the good you do as a mother. And consider ways you can increase your one-on-one time chunks with your children, as well as their daily "mini loves."

UNOFFICIAL LIFE LESSONS

I signed my two toddlers up for a lovely music class. The same class, the same hour. It looked lovely. The teacher was lovely and the curriculum was lovely also. I thought, *What an ideal setup.* Later I thought, *What an ideal migraine.*

While the other moms sat quietly, I bobbed up and down like a kangaroo, not to the music but chasing after my children (I didn't know they had to stay in the circle). Others languidly watched their children clap, hop, dig, and even lunge in time to the music. I felt as if I wore a neon sticker saying Major Mother Loser who can't get her children to dance on cue because she gave them cereal for dinner during one entire summer.

As I sat there, confidently smiling, then stone-faced as I fought thoughts of duct taping my child to the piano—I felt my self-esteem start to shake, then rattle, and finally roll over and play dead. Thankfully, a bludgeon to the head from a flying xylophone mallet brought me to my senses. I thanked the talented teacher, swept up my kids and said, "Park!" Off we went to a nearby park with blazing sun, blue sky, and wide open running spaces.

In *Ten Things I Wish I'd Known Before I Went Out Into the Real World,* Maria Shriver shares, "Kids teach you things about yourself you couldn't learn on your own—lessons about patience and selflessness ... my children have taught me to let things roll off my back ..."

175

Learning does not *only* take place in an official class (for children or parents, for that matter). We buzz children to soccer, piano, swimming, and T-ball, certain we must give them every opportunity available. And indeed there are more opportunities available today than ever before. But more does not always signify better. One tired girl involved in many after school functions told her principal she was so busy because her mom didn't want her around. The principal knew her parents and that this wasn't so, but somehow this little girl didn't get the message.

I have heard women bemoan their budget, and their anxiety at not providing all they, or the neighbors, feel they should. One woman considered an at-home job solely to pay for additional lessons. When guilt comes to shove and anxiety prevails, perhaps spending unstructured "teaching" time casually dancing/singing/playing may be more ideal. And know that spending time with our children—although not penciled in a planner—has meaning that cannot be choreographed.

This is not a picket against structured lessons, by any means. I tried teaching my son piano, thinking we were the perfect match (I play the piano; he wanted to play the piano ...). I was pitifully wrong. But perhaps talking to your child about what they like and how they want to do it may be enlightening. What may be missed in overscheduled structured lessons is the chance for parent and child to learn life's lessons in the most subtle ways.

As with all things, balance is the rose with the thorn. In the end whichever way is best, parents feel relieved knowing that every day they are teaching and growing their children no matter the summer schedule. After that morning—running all over the grassy park—I heard music in my children's laughter and realized they were still living, loving, and learning, even if they weren't in a class.

HOW WOULD YOUR CHILDREN RATE YOUR PARENTING?

Recently, a thought occurred to me—how do our children feel we're doing as parents? We're a fairly normal family with typical issues and stresses. We love each other (generally), get along (mostly), and don't physically harm one another (unless it's wrestling). Usually I'm a happy mother except maybe first thing in the morning. Or late afternoon without a snack. And possibly right before bedtime. But our policy is, when the children graduate they'll get $3,000 for therapy and we'll call it good.

However, to be sure we addressed vital parental elements now, I typed a brief survey of things I wanted to know about how our children perceived our parenting. Things like, do they feel loved by what we say or do, do we spend enough time with them, trust them to do difficult things, or make it easy to tell us when they've done wrong? After finishing the survey I wisely involved my husband so there would be *both* a Mom and Dad questionnaire, to see who the kids really liked best.

I was stunned with the results.

On a scale of 1 to 5 (one being the lowest), from six children, we received a total of nine 3s and 2s. What? After the time and energy we put into our children, subconsciously I had hoped to see a higher Olympic score. But thankfully, the specific information they shared was helpful, and surprising. Like, the children I thought would say we didn't spend enough time with them had zero problem with that. And the one we had pegged as a golden child actually shared an unexpected problem, which led to a fabulously connected discussion, which averted future potential trauma.

To encourage the most honest responses I designed the survey to be done anonymously. So naturally afterward my husband and I pored over the way numbers were circled or crossed out to decipher who felt what. I'm happy to report we were 100% accurate in identifying each child. Although we stink at some parenting concepts—like allowing them to do grown up things—we apparently excel at handwriting analysis.

To begin correcting some of our parenting faux pas, my husband and I both chose a child and privately spoke with them. My teenage son said to me that since I'd had a baby he had missed the two of us just talking, and suggested we take a drive at night and talked for 15 minutes. What an inspired plan. I was encouraged that he not only suggested it, but that he still wanted to connect. After one particularly late evening he asked me about the drive and I replied that I was too exhausted but could we chat in my room? He paused, thinking. "Well," he said, "you're tired, so we can wait until tomorrow." The penny dropped. Yes, he was more interested in the opportunity to drive than to talk though the two-fer was a perk.

Ah, the brutal truths of parenting.

All in all, the survey has been helpful. And my parenting has improved, mainly because right after the survey it became so very bad. I realized it wasn't that I had regressed, it was that I had become more aware. I'm happy to say that I've taken it one step at a time and improved one circled number in a few areas (most especially the one about having a late afternoon snack).

Just for fun try a parenting survey. Keep it anonymous, unlock your inner Sherlock Holmes to decipher their handwriting, and possibly choose one thing to improve. I would write more but it's time for a drive.

JUMPSTART STRONGER FAMILY CONNECTIONS

Between children's sports, dance classes, homework, and playtime, family connection can be tough to find. Try these ideas to create pockets of time and predictable places where you can consistently connect.

Use driving time. Despite your children's protests, this is vital time to get scoops on the day. Turn off the radio and require all ear buds out. Avoid the usual questions of "How was your day?" and instead ask specifics— "Who did you hang with at lunch/play with at recess? What was the high/low today?" Then ask follow up questions—"Why?" or "What did he say?" or "What did you do about it?" No need to make it an interrogating interview, but a few follow-up questions yields great info nuggets that can come in handy later. And keep the gasps and judgment calls for later. The more you can validate your child's feelings and experiences (even if you don't agree), the more likely they'll share the meatier stuff.

Establish a "chat room." In your home or car, on the back deck or at the kitchen counter, create a usual place to talk where they know you'll likely be. My children know that after an evening activity mom will most likely be in her pj's, in her bed, lamp on, journal in hand, waiting for a lowdown on the fun. When my kids return from an activity, I love hearing the door open and close, then the thump of feet on the stairs heading right to my room. Wherever you choose, make it a lovely place with things that invite warmth—milk and cookies in the kitchen, a cozy chair in your bedroom—and you'll find they want to be there too.

Choose "their" night. Specifically and clearly choose a consistent time to spend individually with each child. It doesn't matter the frequency—once a month, every other day. Or the time frame—pop in for a surprise lunch, on the way to volleyball, etc. These one-on-one times are tough to choreograph but so fabulously worth it. In our family, where else would I hear the vital details of the latest Rick Riordan book, or the intense playground drama I'd only guessed at? It doesn't always have to be "a deal." Driving one of my daughters to her dance class is a perfect time to pair it with a Subway dinner once in a while. We typically alternate the duration of activities—a full-on dinner, brief ice cream at the park, or a dollar movie and popcorn (driving at least thirty minutes to get there so we can talk on the way).

Keep connection simple but meaningful. Ideally, try to involve their interests. My one son and I attended many of the Harry Potter book releases (and ate Bertie Botts beans at midnight). He still talked about this even when he went to college. Every attempt—even board games in a child's room with you, him, and a root beer—helps children feel "I matter."

Choose one way this week to add zest and connection to face time with your family!

LEARN TO SPEAK YOUR CHILD'S LOVE LANGUAGE

A few years ago I noticed a shift in my fourth-grade son. Typically talkative, he had become slightly withdrawn, moody, and less himself. Ironically—and thankfully—at the time I was reading Gary Chapman's *The Five Love Languages of Children*. After thinking about his personality, I felt to do more verbal and physical languages. When we talked about his school day I mussed his hair, rubbed his shoulder, or simply touched his arm. Within a few days, I couldn't believe the difference—he was back to himself.

A small shift in the way we "speak" our child's love language can immediately make a difference. And yet, what we do doesn't have to be dramatic. A few minutes daily of showing love how they best receive it can bring big results. Dr. Chapman's five key areas include physical touch, words of affirmation, quality time, gifts, and acts of service.

First, consider a child that's concerning you. Which of those love languages do they most resonate with? Likely, there will be at least one or two. Then choose a simple action you can do to jumpstart change. Several of my children like words of affirmation, but I've found a mix of verbal and written best. I bought bright red mini mailboxes, tiny little things but big enough for an index card and a treat. Now displayed in our front room they are perfect for a weekly note, scripture card of the day, or tasty treat. My children—even the older ones—look for the upright mailbox flags that show, "You've got mail." It's fast for me and meaningful for them.

For those children more electronically focused, I also text a favorite scripture, quick quote, or loving thought—"Hey, sure appreciate that you caught up on homework." Words of affirmation simply say, "I want to connect with you."

After determining the language and some simple actions, stay with it for a week or two. Forget filing and cleaning out the cabinets—allow this to be priority one. Watch for changes or things you may need to do differently for a better result. As our children got older I noticed my husband and I had less individual time with them. So we opted for more "quality time" by creating Gender Nights and Date Nights. On the former, my husband would take the boys to their kind of fun (sweaty, action-packed, involving some kind of sport), and I would take the girls to theirs (delicious, shopping-packed, involving some kind of park). Then he and I would rotate through the six children for an individual Date Night. It wasn't weekly but at least every other so that within weeks we had both spent a dinner, or at least an ice cream and a chat with each child. This one consistent action alone has kept us close to our children and more in the know about the details of their lives.

Love languages truly work. Take a few minutes and think about your children and their particular love language. Consider a simple action you can start, and then do it for at least a week. And you might be surprised that in doing so, your love languages are more often spoken from simply and more consciously speaking theirs.

ABOUT THE AUTHOR

Connie Sokol is a mother of seven, a local and national presenter, and a contributor on KSL TV's "Studio 5" and "Motherhood Matters" blog. Mrs. Sokol is the author of several books including *Create a Powerful Life Plan, Motherhood Matters, Faithful, Fit & Fabulous*, and the romance, *Caribbean Crossroads*. Mrs. Sokol marinates in time spent with her family and eating decadent treats. For blog posts, podcasts, products and more, visit www.conniesokol.com.